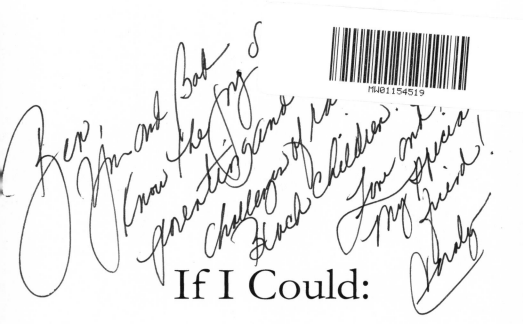

If I Could:

Lessons for Navigating an Unjust World

Kelisa JaVon Wing

Foreword by Sharif El-Mekki

Books by Kelisa Wing

Conversations

Weeds & Seeds:
How to Stay Positive in the Midst of Life's Storms

Promises & Possibilities:
Dismantling the School-to-Prison Pipeline

If I Could: Lessons for Navigating an Unjust World

CONTENTS

DEDICATION

For Naima and Jadon

Foreword: by Sharif El-Mekki

History is not the past. It is the present. We carry our history with us. We are our history. - James Baldwin

It was a blessing to hear the words of Kelisa Wing—an amazing teacher, a curator of history, a masterful storyteller, and a truth-telling activist and revolutionary—as I listened to the first chapter of *If I Could: Lessons for Navigating an Unjust World*.

What I heard was a truth that, despite my intimate familiarity with what Black children experience in America, felt like a succession of massive bolo punches. America's sins aren't in the past because history is never in the past. It's relived and recreated. In this book, Kelisa is holding up a mirror to America and penning a searing note to its most privileged citizens – as well as to its most vulnerable.

Our racial trauma is displayed and replayed. The rage, racial stress, and despair as we continue to see state-sanctioned murder play out beyond the huddled whispers and speeches of our ancestors. Today, executions of Black, Brown, and Native people aren't just in the woods and barns, they're on Bay Street on Staten Island, in the lot of the Cudell Recreation Center in Cleveland, on Canfield Drive in Ferguson, and where Larpenteur Avenue and Fry Street intersect in the Twin Cities.

Our children and youth are bombarded with messages of Black, Brown, and Native people being worth less and worthless. All children, especially white children, are constantly exposed to messages of subtle and overt white supremacy. And, while institutional racism deserves our full attention, we cannot ignore the day-to-day messages sent and received as many racist mindsets

9

are taught and reinforced at people's dining room tables, during their car rides home, and in their classrooms and schools.

As educators, we are not just here to teach content, we have to ensure the safety of our children—not just physically, but also intellectually, culturally, emotionally, and spiritually.

How do we do that? We do that by using education as a path towards freedom. Some may think that we are already free, but not all of us are. If you are Black in America, you have been liberated, but you may not yet be free. True freedom isn't just *freedom to* pursue your dreams, it is *freedom from* the racist, bigoted, and biased mindsets that fetter and derail our children's dreams and perceptions of who they are.

We know that Black children experience racial bias from their teachers as early as pre-K. And that's from educators, who in America, are supposed to be the *good guys*. What do our youth experience from overt racists?

The revolutionaries we need in our schools and classrooms plan for the realities our communities face and are fueled by hope and love for our people. In the face of massive inequity and pervasive apathy, Kelisa provides anecdotes and reflections that inspire and teach.

You may experience searing pain while reading this book, but you won't despair because Kelisa gives us a blueprint—a freedom quilt, if you will—to chart a path forward and upward. Mama Zora Neale Hurston taught us that *if you are silent about your pain, they'll kill you and say you enjoyed it.*

As Black people, we can take no solace that America will act without being constantly confronted, taught forcefully and effectively. Kelisa clearly, fully, and deliberately provides that for us. I am grateful to her for laying bare her experiences, as painful as they are, because silence never supports the victims, only the oppressors.

10

May we all be brave enough to enact what she teaches us and never remain silent about pain—especially that of our children.

Sharif El-Mekki is the Founder and CEO of the Center for Black Educator Development. The Center exists to ensure there will be equity in the recruiting, training, hiring, and retention of quality educators that reflect the cultural backgrounds and share common socio-political interests of the students they serve.

The Center is developing a nationally relevant model to measurably increase teacher diversity and support Black educators through four pillars: Professional learning, Pipeline, Policies, and Pedagogy. So far, the Center has developed ongoing and direct professional learning and coaching opportunities for Black teachers and other educators serving students of color.

The Center also carries forth the freedom or liberation school legacy by hosting a Freedom School that incorporates research-based curricula and exposes high school and college students to the teaching profession to help fuel a pipeline of Black educators.

Prior to founding the Center, El-Mekki served as a nationally recognized principal and U.S. Department of Education Principal Ambassador Fellow.

El-Mekki's school, Mastery Charter Shoemaker, was recognized by President Obama and Oprah Winfrey, and was awarded the prestigious EPIC award for three consecutive years as being amongst the top three schools in the country for accelerating students' achievement levels.

The Shoemaker Campus was also recognized as one of the top ten middle school and top ten high schools in the state of Pennsylvania for accelerating the achievement levels of African-American students.

El-Mekki is also the founder of the Fellowship: Black Male Educators for Social Justice, an organization dedicated to recruiting, retaining, and developing Black male teachers.

El-Mekki blogs on Phillys7thWard, is a member of the 8 Black Hands podcast and serves on several boards and committees focused on educational and racial justice.

PREFACE

In the past few years since you came into this world, a lot has been happening. I started to take notice when you were in my womb in 2005 and Hurricane Katrina was playing out before the world's eyes. We were elated in 2008 when we elected our first Black President and believed change has come! However, since then, many Black people have been murdered by police officers with no recourse, each one paining me as a mother, a Black woman, and a human more and more.

The President who followed behind our change maker brought division, hatred, and confusion. I found myself having to have conversations with you all that I never imagined I would have to as mother - conversations that my parents never had to have with us. As each tragedy happened, new approaches had to occur, as to how to protect your innocence, and, at the same time, make you aware of the world that is out there. The world that could claim you if you were not cognizant and alert.

When I was a little girl, my mother always used to play "If I Could" by Regina Belle for us. She would hold our little hands in hers and sing so beautifully the words,

If I Could, I would protect you from the sadness in your eyes – give you courage in a world of compromise, yes I would, if I could.

Tears streaming down her face, she would sing each verse with more veracity than the last. I didn't quite understand all of the meaning of the song, but I did know that my mother loved us and was, through this song in particular, conveying the sentiment that she would do anything for us. I never fully understood the love your Nana had for us until I became a mother.

She continued on,

If I could, I would try to shield your innocence from time, but the part of life I gave you isn't mine. I'll watch you grow, so I could let you go, it was at this point in the song that Nana would squeeze our hand the tightest, and her tears would fall like rain.

And now that I am your mother, I now know; I now understand that you are always mine, but one day you will go. So before that day comes, I want to share a few things with you.

14

Part I:

Injustice Anywhere is a Threat to Justice Everywhere

Part I: Injustice Anywhere is a Threat to Justice Everywhere

One of my favorite quotes in life has been,

Injustice anywhere is a threat to justice everywhere – Martin
Luther King, Jr.

I have tried to pass this belief onto you both throughout the years
through the example of not only my words, but the way I live my
life. Both of you have endured the sacrifice of my absence in the
name of equity. Since 2016, I have been gone 1-2 times a month
either speaking or presenting somewhere to educate others on
equity, social justice, and dismantling disparate systems.

I have gotten angry at you when I believed that you were allowing
others to walk over you, especially those who were abusing their
privilege.

I saw the pain in your eyes as I spoke up for you at laser tag when
a group of white children cut you both in line with no regard.

"Mom, it's okay," You both said half pleading half embarrassed.

"No, it is not okay. You teach people how to treat you." I said in a
scolding manner.

I want you both to always advocate for yourself and for others
when there are injustices happening.

17

I was not sure when the right time was to start to talk with you both about the world in which you were a part of, but the world decided that for me.

On July 7, 2016, we were just waking up in our hotel room. I was so excited to be in Florida and ready to begin the day. Looking out the window, I could not help but think about how blessed we were as a family to be able to give you the life experiences that we never had.

In the middle of my thoughts, I was pulled out of my feelings by the newscaster on CNN,

"The footage you are about to see is disturbing and not appropriate for children."

As I turned around to face the TV, I saw a Facebook live video of a Black man, later identified on CNN as Philando Castile, taking his last breath in front of his girlfriend and her daughter because a police officer decided that his life did not matter that day. Listening to the wallowing cries of his girlfriend haunts me to this day.

I felt a tightness in my chest and grabbed for it with one hand as I covered my mouth with the other. *Another one* I thought as I felt the tears sting the corner of my eyes. Just one day prior, Alton Sterling was murdered in Louisiana. He was the 114th Black man killed in the United States in 2016, and it was only July (Riotta, 2016).

Oblivious to the situation, all you guys cared about was getting to the pool as your father and I quickly shut the television off. You were only 4 and 11 years old, and this was something we never really had to contend with while we were growing up.

When I was your age, I was called a nigger and discriminated against, but I never worried about losing my life as a kid. With each new police shooting, I grew more and more afraid for you guys.

I quietly went into the bathroom, punched the air, and cried until I gasped for air, as I thought *not again*. It could have been my father, my mother, my brother, my sister, my son, my daughter, my husband....me. I wiped my tears, bit my bottom lip, and put on a brave face for you guys. We went down to the pool to enjoy the Florida sun, although my heart hurt thinking about it all.

Sitting in a lounge chair, I started to notice a white woman who was sitting on the side of the pool with her legs dangling in the water. You guys were on the other side of the pool with your dad, but for some reason, I sensed something was awry with the woman. She continually looked with disdain at a little Black girl who was enjoying the warm sun while seeming to not mind the raucous that two little white boys were creating nearby.

"She needs to stay over there," I heard her whisper to her partner.

This beautiful little Black girl, who could not have been more than five or six years old, was enjoying a great time at the pool. She was being a typical little girl, but unfortunately for Black children, many times they are held to a different standard than most children. As the little girl was playing in the pool, she splashed water everywhere, inadvertently hitting the white woman.

"Get away from me! You people never control your kids!," The white woman angrily said to the little girl and her father who sat nearby.

I sat up erect.

19

"Excuse me ma'am, *you people* who are you calling you people!!"
I said as my voice shook from the anger that lingered inside of me
just beneath the surface of trying to stay calm.

"Oh don't go there," she said waving me away with the flick of her
wrist.

"No ma'am, I will go there. I have sat here and watched you be
mean spirited to this baby for the past 20 minutes, all the while
those little boys have been playing in the same fashion and you
have said absolutely nothing to them!"

At the same time, the little girl's father came over to see what was
happening.

"If she did something wrong, I apologize," he sincerely said.

"You *better* apologize and control her. She is acting like an
animal." She then continued to shout at the little girl and her father
for a few more minutes.

I was livid. I had heard enough and seen enough, and I was
emotionally done. It was distinct what was happening right in front
of my eyes, hours after Philando Castile and Alton Sterling were
brutally murdered for no reason at all – their skin color, deemed
sinister, was, and still is, not a crime!

"Get out of the pool," I said to you guys, to a chorus of, "But
why?"

"Come, sit down." I said as your father and you all sat down at a
table away from the pool.

"I want you to know, that if we could, we would protect you from
everything that could harm you in this world," I paused fighting
back tears, "but unfortunately, today had shown us that we

20

cannot."

"What that woman just did, it was racist," I said to you as I took a deep breath.

You looked confused as I continued to talk,

"Some people are going to hate you because of the color of your skin. That woman, what she did," I choked back tears, "it was wrong, but it is something you will face in your lives. We want you to be ready."

Your father continued to talk with you as well, reassuring you that it won't be your fault, and that it is their issue, not yours.

"I want to tell you something, a man, he was killed yesterday because of the color of his skin by the police. We want to tell you what to do if you are ever stopped by the police."

"Yes ma'am," you all said with fear in your voice.

It hurts to think back to this moment, but I told you guys to be acquiescent.

"Make no sudden moves, keep your hands in sight, and, above all, do whatever they ask you to do. Because they can take your life, and I don't know what we would do if something ever happened to you guys," I said as I wiped away my tears and embraced you all.

I don't know if I told you the right thing, but there was no guide to the hate we were experiencing. I thought back to our ancestors and wondered what kinds of conversations they had to have with their children.

In that moment, I wondered if Emmett Till's mother told him to be compliant. Did she warn her son to not look at white women in the eyes? Did she tell him about the lies that can kill him if he did not "act accordingly"? Did it even matter?

As we learned in 2017, the woman who said he whistled at her; the woman responsible for having him drug from his sleep, stripped naked, made to carry a part of a cotton gin, beaten, eye extracted from the socket, shot execution style, and tossing his young Black body into the Tallahatchie River in Mississippi (History, 2010), admitted that she lied.

How can we protect you from a lie? *Did Mamie Till's warning help Emmitt? Would mine help you?* I prayed to God it would. In my mind, the shootings of Black people in this century is no different than the lynching of Black bodies in the last century. I wonder, will it ever end?

It was 2016, and we were nearing the end of the Obama era. It seemed that at the end of his term, we saw the true colors of the nation shining through.

I remember conducting a lesson with my students where we were studying whether or not a candidate was responsible for the way their attendees acted. It was tough to see people spitting on people of color and a candidate encouraging violence against people who held beliefs that were opposite to their own. We had never seen such a thing in the political arena. Oh how far we had gone from the unified cries of "yes we can".

Much of what shaped my desire to advocate for others started in the 1980s. Being the only Black family in the neighborhood brought about many forms of racism in all of her fury and monstrosity.

Whether it was being told to go back to Africa, to get off of "their" side of the street, or being beat up by the street bully for, as she called it, "being a dirty little nigger", I had to fight.

After that talk, we have had to have some very profound conversations. I have struggled to put things into words that you could comprehend in your young minds and, at the same time, wanted you to not live in fear.

My heart broke last week when you told me you were scared to move away from home because you feared the gun violence that plagues this country. The gun violence this country refuses to deal with.

Etched into my mind was April 20, 1999, my senior year. We were driving to a choir concert, and on the radio, I heard the news of two students committing a mass shooting at this high school. I had never heard of such loss of life at the hands of students at a place that we felt like we could feel safe at. I thought for sure the government would do something about gun violence – that was 20 years ago.

I believed with all of my heart that after Sandy Hook, something would have changed. It nearly took my breath away when my principal stopped by my classroom to check on *me* because someone burst into a school building and slaughtered innocent children and educators. *Check on me?* I wondered why this country was not checking on gun control.

The same gun violence that allowed a racist to enter a prayer service in South Carolina and kill people as they fellowshipped and worshipped together for no other reason than for the color of their skin. For the first time, if I saw visitors at church, I would wonder if they meant us harm or if they were there to worship with us.

The same gun violence that took lives in Parkland. This time, I thought, they are finally going to act because the children used their pain to advocate for the change that most of the people in this country sought. They marched, protested, sat in the offices of Congressional members, and in 2018, a gun violence reform bill was passed in the House, but the Senate refuses to act because the Senate Majority Leader cares more about staying in the good graces of the NRA than he does protecting our children.

The same gun violence that led a racist into a Walmart in El Paso, Texas this past summer. I cried for weeks. You both watched me this time fully understanding what was happening.

I hugged you tighter, held you longer, and prayed with more fervor that you both would be okay. I knew that the mass shooting in Texas affected me more than any other one when I sat in the parking lot of our local Walmart feeling my heart beating as if it was about to explode out of my chest, palms sweating, gasping for air, afraid to enter the store. All I could do was pray because I felt helpless to put one foot in front of the other to walk into that store without the faith that everything was going to be alright. You should not feel like you are taking a risk by going into a store, going to school, or worshipping at church.

The gun violence that took lives in Dayton, Ohio not even a few days after El Paso – when, please tell me, when will this end?!?

The gun violence that took Nekitto from our family in 1992. My oldest male cousin; your cousin that you never got the opportunity to meet. I often think about his 15 years of life. Too young to die. So much life behind his eyes. They say the eyes are the windows to the soul; that you can see people for who they really are through their eyes.

Nekitto was full of life, joy, happiness – he was light and the embodiment of Black boy joy. For years, I would cry at the thought of what might have been, what could have been, what

24

should have been. He should be here today. Instead, a bullet robbed him of his youth, time, future, goals, plans, and stole our tomorrow.

All we have left is memories. His death never made the evening news, but for us, it was as if time stood still and nothing else mattered. The void was deep and gaping. The world was robbed of his presence, talent, love; his seed – his legacy.

This is the world you are living in – and I need for you to be fully aware of it all – the splendor and the cruelty the opportunities and the obstacles, so you can be ready.

Matthew 10:16 *Behold, I send you forth as a sheep in the midst of wolves: be ye therefore wise as serpents, and harmless as doves*

I want to explain things from the beginning though, what led us here to where we are today. It started in 2005.

Part II: The Gift

Part II: The Gift

When I was younger, I never pictured myself as a mother. I wasn't interested in being domesticated. Your Nana would call me into the kitchen to teach me how to cook, and I resisted. I watched the way Nana catered to our family, to your grandfather, and I saw it as a sign of weakness. As I have gotten older, I realized that she was the backbone of our family. Her strength was not loud or boisterous, but quiet, resolute, and powerful.

**

Lesson 1: You do not have to be the biggest and loudest person in the room. Remember that more is caught than taught, so what is done is much more important than what is spoken. Believe 90% of what you see and 10% of what you hear.

**

Nana was calm, peaceful, and loving in the face of adversity and strife. What I viewed as a weakness in my youth, I see as strength in my adulthood.

I wasn't interested in cooking because I did not think I would get married or become a mother. The funny thing is now you both are here and cooking is something I absolutely love.

**

Lesson 2: Two words you should not say: 'never' and 'always'. When you find yourself in a disagreement, don't tell someone "you never do this" or "you always do that" because it implies something that is not true. Someone does not always or never do something. Also, do not put limitations on your life by saying you cannot do something. The power of life and death over a situation depends on what you say about it. If you say never, you never will. If you say you can, you will be able to do anything.

**

When we found out we were going to have you, it was something we planned through another situation.

A month before we got pregnant with you, I shared with your father my fear that I was pregnant. Sure, we were married, but we thought we would start a family a few years later. I had a career in the United States Army and was slated to become a Drill Sergeant. Your father and I were stationed in two different places, so a child was not in our plans.

I remember being so nervous waiting to find out if I was with child. I thought, *I'm not ready to be a mom.* All kinds of thoughts raced through my mind, but then, I found out I was not pregnant. Something happened that I did not expect. My heart was broken, and I was disappointed.

**

Lesson 3: Disappointment. In life you will be disappointed. You will face disappointments as children, teenagers, adults, and in your older age. The thing about disappointment is that in order to

29

go through it in a way that won't crush your spirit is to remember that the root of disappointment is 'dis' which means not and appoint means time. So remember with disappointment it simply means it is not your time, but if it is meant to be, someday it will be. Stay positive.

**

When your father saw how sad I was, he said,

"Maybe we should try to have a baby and see what happens".

We did, and two weeks later, we were pregnant with you. I could not have been happier. I remember the night I learned I was having you. I laid down in my bed and prayed to God about your life. I said,

"Lord, I am praying for a healthy baby, but Lord, if you would consider, I would like to ask you for a daughter."

Mind you, I was happy regardless just to be pregnant, but I had such a wonderful relationship with your Nana, and I wanted that with you.

I never quite knew that I could love someone as much as I loved you, and I had not even met you.

In May, we heard your heartbeat for the first time, and I learned that God answered my prayers – you were a girl!

One day, your dad came home from work and I was crying.

"What's wrong honey?" He asked.

I admitted that I was afraid of our future and our ability to push through hard times.

**

Lesson 4: Marriage is hard work. When, and if, you both get married, understand that in today's society, remaining together will be tough. In your vows, remember that a three string cord represents you, your partner, and God. When you allow God to be at the center of your life and your marriage, He can take the ordinary and make it extraordinary; He can take the impossible and make it possible.

As much as people in our generation are so quick to walk away and give up, my hope for you both is that you will endure and persevere, not just in marriage, should you get married, but in life. Through the struggle, you grow the most. In discomfort (dis=not), we grow so much. Don't shy away from hard things and don't give up so quickly.

**

I explained to your father that I didn't want to hurt you and be the cause of you growing up in a single parent home. We were scared; we both came from an upbringing where our parents' relationships did not survive.

The pain of growing up without a father is an inexplicable pain that I struggle to articulate in words and on paper. It felt like a hole that was unfillable, a constant dark cloud that hung over my head. The first man that loved me, that was supposed to love me, was missing in my life, and I struggled to not feel like something was wrong with me.

As a result, I made a lot of poor decisions in my life, and, not just in my romantic relationships, but in all relationships, in which I hung on to toxic connections for way too long and made concessions for people who did not deserve it at all because I was

31

looking for the love of a father. I did not want that for either of you. I do not want it for any child.

Your father and I, while you were not yet born, but in my womb, decided that we would do our very best to stay together. As our oldest, I know you have seen a lot and heard a lot. I have watched tears fall down your face and heard the worry in your voice when your father and I have gone through tough times. I want you to understand why we stayed and endured through the tough times. Why we chose to stay – I could say a number of reasons, but back in 2005, we promised to do it for you so that we could give you what we did not have. We wanted to break a generational curse.

The thing is, in your life, we saw God's promise of love and hope. We didn't even understand the promise completely that we made then, but as I reflect on it now, I am thankful we did.

My pregnancy with you was easy and calm, but your birth was traumatic. It was Thanksgiving day, and you were already almost a week late. We had resolved that we were going to be eating dinner that day and that you would come when you were good and ready to, much like now ☺.

Prior to my pregnancy with you, I never really paid attention to crimes against children, but it seemed that every day on the news there was some innocent child being abused or being violated in ways that no human should be. I grew very protective of you, shielding my womb from any and everything, and wishing you could stay there forever in order to keep you from the evil of the world. At the same time, I was conflicted because for all of the evil in the world, there was beauty there too.

The way the leaves change from green to yellow at the passing of the season, and the way that those same leaves fall from the trees in autumn. The crunching sound of those leaves under your feet, the smell of the air as the season changes from autumn to winter, and the melting of a snowflake on your cheek. The way a single dew drop hangs from a flower petal, as if gravity suspends, if but only for an instant, right before it hits the cold grass. The way the sun looks right before it rises as it sits still on the horizon, its glow illuminating the sky. A representation of God's promise of a new day, a fresh start, beginning again. The peaceful quiet after a ravenous storm. A placid voice in a loud room. The aroma of my mother's cooking as I walked in the house after school. There is beauty all around us – we just have to find it.

**

Lesson 5: Life is all about perspective. For all that is bad, there is good. Nothing is ever one way. I know there will be things that come along to rock your world and test your faith in humanity, but remain steadfast and immoveable. You cannot change the way people are, but you can control how you respond to them. You can control your behavior, and you can choose to remain positive. Apostle Lyndon Townsend reminds us that if you cannot change the state you are in, you can change the *state* you are in. You can choose how you look at life. You can view everything as bad and miss the good stuff, or you can look for the beauty – it is all about your perspective.

**

I will never forget sitting on the bed after a long day at work in August of 2005. You were wildly kicking me like the karate kid as if you were trying to free yourself from within. I was flipping through the channels, and I landed on CNN. They were reporting that a hurricane was coming – her name was Katrina.

I thought this storm would be like all the others that had come before her. Growing up in the 90s, I watched many people survive through Hurricane Andrew, and, while it was a devastating storm, I imagined that would be the worst I would see in my lifetime.

For the next few days, I could not stop watching the news. Once the storm hit, I could not turn away from the devastation. It was hard to believe what I was seeing on the news as I rubbed my stomach. My sense of feeling seemed to intensify after I got pregnant with you.

The lack of resources and the lack of response was unprecedented – I had never seen such a thing in my life. As I write this, I remember thinking that I would never see such a lack of disregard from our government, but I was wrong. As the eye of the hurricane hit, it felt like we were watching something taking place in a 3rd world country.

This could not be happening in America I thought.

How could our people be treated like this?

My heart ached for the senseless loss of life. The most hurtful part of Katrina was knowing that if this storm would have hit a different city, a different ward, people of a different hue, the response would have been different and this would not have occurred.

For weeks, we watched and waited to see what the lasting devastation would be. Sadly, when I visited this past year, there are still parts of New Orleans that have never recovered, and there are people who have never returned. 1,833 people lost their lives to Katrina (CNN Library).

There are moments in a person's life where their thinking shifts based on knowledge, understanding, and an awakening to truth. This was my moment. I had many situations of injustices that I witnessed, but this was the moment when I saw widespread inhumanity on display for the world to see. Although I was a full time college student while pregnant with you and exposed to a great deal of knowledge, I learned more while watching that atrocity than I could ever learn from a book. What I realized was that we, as people of color, are mistreated because of our socioeconomic status and for the color of our skin on a systemic level. I knew that if I could, I would try to keep you from that level of hate and injustice, but the best I can do is to educate you, so you can be prepared for it when it comes because it will come.

I know there are times when you wonder why I am so passionate about talking about issues that impact people of color. It began when I was called a 'nigger' when I was younger than your brother currently is; I was 6 years old. I went home and asked your grandfather what that word meant.

"Fight," was his response to my question. *Fight* is what he wanted me to do from then on if I was called that word again, and fight I did – fight I have!

I fought just about every day that we lived in that neighborhood. At the time, all I knew was how to fight with my hands. As time has gone on and life has been the ultimate teacher, I have learned to fight with my writing; I fight with my knowledge; I fight with my words; I fight by keeping you informed and aware of injustice so that you can fight too, not with your hands, but with your mind.

While my upbringing, learning, and experiences have shaped me into who I am today, the seed was planted for me to be an advocate for equity on a broader scale while you were in my womb as I watched Katrina. I never want you to be a bystander. Elie Wiesel, author of *Night* in his Nobel Peace Prize acceptance speech said,

We must always take sides. Neutrality helps the oppressor,

35

never the victim. Silence encourages the tormentor, never the tormented. Sometimes we must interfere. When human lives are endangered, when human dignity is in jeopardy, national borders and sensitivities become irrelevant. Wherever men or women are persecuted because of their race, religion, or political views, that place must—at that moment—become the center of the universe (Reilly, 2016).

I wanted to be a voice for the voiceless, and I hope that as you grow up, you will use your voice against injustice as well.

**

Lesson 6: *Know from whence you came.* I want you to always know about those who have come before you. Remember that our ancestors survived the Middle Passage in the underbelly of a slave ship whipped and chained together, naked, afraid, and hungry. Those who survived the horrific journey were ushered off of the boat like cattle and treated, not as humans, but as property.

Our ancestors stood on auction blocks and were sold to the highest bidder. Children were savagely ripped from the arms of their mothers, and families were separated never to be seen again. All the while, your ancestors could not fully understand what was happening, as they did not speak the language in this new country that they were brought to. They took on new names, had to abandon their culture, their religion, and their freedom. This went on for over 400 years.

After our ancestors survived slavery, they had to deal with *Plessy v. Ferguson* in 1890 and the "separate but equal" laws that followed and encouraged widespread legalized racism across this nation (Packard, 2002). Our ancestors survived this too then fought for Civil Rights, achieved them, and here we stand today almost in the year 2020.

I share all of this with you because when you think you cannot go on, when you think something is too hard, I want to remind you of the blood that is flowing through your veins. You come from conflict, survival, stick-to-itiveness, perseverance, and endurance. You were formed and birthed through the struggle. Your ancestors survived ALL of that for you to be here, not making excuses, but for you to be paving the way for those who will come after you.

You were born with a purpose, and you owe it to your ancestors to live life boldly, to give everything your all, and to persevere through every obstacle and challenge that will come your way. You are the ancestors of those not yet born; what legacy will you create for them?

It never left me when I was the age you are now, that your great-grandfather told me of his struggle living in Atlanta as a young Black man running home one day from the Ku Klux Klan. As I sat there listening to him, I wondered what would have happened if he had not outrun them that day. If he would have become "strange fruit" hanging from a tree, and there would be no Nana, no me, no you – our legacy, like the legacies of the 3,446 Black bodies that were lynched between 1882-1968 (NAACP, 2019) for simply being Black, would have been cut short. We are still here, and your great-grandfather is still here at 92 years old to tell his story to me so that I can pass it on to you.

**

I was not surprised at how long it took for you to make your entrance in this world. Back then, just as today, you tend to move at your own pace although you know that your father and I want you to move with a purpose. The idea of moving with a purpose is something we both learned as soldiers in the United States Army. We understood that being on time meant the difference between life and death in the service and that we were obligated to something much bigger than ourselves. Other people were depending on us to be on time.

You think when we implore you to be on time that we are simply nagging you, but we want you to understand that timeliness is important. There are appointed places in life that you are preordained to be at, but it starts with your ability to be there at the appointed time.

I was the only person on the maternity ward the night I went into labor. I was in more pain than I have ever felt in my life, and with each minute, the pain seemed to intensify. After 10 hours of labor, the doctor came in and explained that you were under duress, and that if something did not happen soon, we were going to need to have a cesarean. I was so terrified. After a few more hours, the doctor came back in the room and said that your heart rate was now increasing, and we could not wait any longer.

I was in the operating room, and I felt like a failure. I could not even push you into the world – something that I was told as a woman I should have been able to do – I could not do. I did not dilate enough to safely deliver you, so you began to retreat back into the safety of my womb.

After the doctors strapped me down to the gurney, the operating door asked,

"Can you feel this," as he ran his fingers over my stomach.

"Yes," at which time he immediately began to cut me with no regard to my response.

I cried, screamed, and looked at your father in shock as he cut me further, deeper, and with more intensity.

"This is not supposed to be happening! Can't you see that she is pain?," your father said as he questioned and pleaded with the anesthesiologist.

She explained to him that there was nothing she could do for me since I was already cut open.

I fought so hard that I ripped my strapped down arm from the gurney as the anesthesiologist tried to pin it back down. I felt every tear, every tug, every pull the doctors performed as they tried to free your 8 lb. 8 oz. body from a six inch cut to my abdomen.

And then, you cried and took your first breath – inhaled from the world into your lungs and exhaled your first sound. It was the most beautiful sound I had ever heard in my life.

When they showed you to me, I have to admit, I was angry. Not because you were here, but because of the excruciating pain that I was in because of their failure to take care with your birth.

As soon as you were free from my body, as promised, the anesthesiologist gave me medicine that took my pain away, but the trauma of it all was engrained in my mind for the rest of my life.

As they wheeled me from the operating room to my hospital room, I overheard the doctor tell your father, "She will have to have all her children by cesarean," and, before I drifted into a deep medicine induced sleep, I whispered through tears, "I will under no circumstances have any more children."

For the next few hours, I drifted in and out of sleep. Each time I opened my eyes, I saw your father with you, holding you, kissing you, and nurturing you. You spent the first six hours of your life bonding with your father because I was too out of to do anything but sleep.

One time, I woke up and heard him promising you that he would always look out for you, always take care of you, and that he would always love you. A nurse eventually came in and told me that if I wanted to nurse you, I would have to do it soon or they would feed you a bottle. Your father, in his infinite wisdom, did a lot of research about the benefits of breast feeding vs. bottle feeding. I was not interested in nursing at all, but your dad was able to convince me that it was the healthiest thing for you.

From the beginning, your father has done what is best for you. I know sometimes you don't see it, but as someone who grew up without my father's presence at the age you are now, I can tell you that you are blessed. I do not think it was a coincidence that the time you spent in your first hours in the world were spent with him.

For the first few days of your life, I felt inadequate. I struggled with post-partum depression and felt like I was less than a woman because I could not deliver you.

As women, we place so many unnecessary pressures upon ourselves, convincing ourselves that we aren't enough. The truth of the matter is – we are enough! As you grow up, I want you to not buy into the lie that you have to prove

40

something.

As a child, I was taught that I had to jump higher, run faster, and be better to prove that I deserved to be where I was. Meanwhile, white parents did not espouse these ideas on their children, and instead, allowed children their innocence and youth. For you, I say just be who God called you to be. Just be you, knowing that you are good enough.

As the weeks passed by, my guilt dissipated, and I knew that I was still a mother and a woman, delivery or not, you were here, healthy, and we were grateful.

The country was still healing from Katrina. I will never forget when Kanye West was on television and he said,

"I hate the way they portray us in the media, if you see a Black family, they say we are looting, and if you see a white family, they say they are looking for food...George Bush doesn't care about Black people" (Terry, 2015), during a red cross telethon.

It was such a shock to hear someone speak about a sitting President in such a way, but it was a wakeup call to the pain that people of color in the country were feeling. People were shocked at how we were treating our own citizens so inhumanely; however, unfortunately, we have always treated people of color and those who were less fortunate in this manner – it was just now being televised for the world to see.

A week or so after your birth, I was able to return to college to take my final exam for microeconomics to earn my Associates degree.

**

Lesson 7: Langston Hughes, one of my favorite poets, said, "Hold fast to dreams. For if dreams die Life is a broken winged bird that cannot fly." No matter what path life leads you to, hold on to your dreams and work feverishly to make your dreams a reality by any means necessary. The only thing that can stand in your way, is you. Nothing is impossible to those who believe – never forget that.

**

Lesson 8: Never stop learning. Learning has always excited me! I have watched you develop a love for knowledge and truth over the years. Never lose that passion and thirst for the acquisition of truth and knowledge because the truth makes us free!

We never get to the point of obtaining it all. As an educator, I've always prided myself on being a lifelong learner, and I hope you esteem to that as well. In this ugly world we are living in where people are quick to accept someone else's perception as reality, we must remember that the courage to seek the truth, to not believe beautiful lies, but to accept hard, sometimes painful, truths is the key to true healing. If I could give you a better version of this thing we call life, I would, but as Tupac said, *I was given this world, I didn't make it.*

Knowledge will always be your power – seize it! For years I continued in school and you emulated me – imitation is the highest form of flattery – and boy was I flattered! I would ask,

"What are you doing?," and you would say,

"My homework!"

Education was like another member of our family – there are moments when I wonder if I have been present enough in your lives in my pursuit of knowledge and providing our family a better life. I worry about those moments when I was not fully there.

The moments when I would be writing a paper on the sidelines of your soccer games; the moments when rather than reading you a developmentally appropriate bedtime story, I would read you my articles or books for school because I needed to complete it for class, or the moments when you wanted to play, but I needed to complete "just one more assignment".

I regret the moments while I watched you and your father bonding while we were on vacation while I sat poolside with a laptop studying. I hope you know it was for you. Not entirely for you – for all of us: for myself, your dad, your brother – although he wasn't here yet – and for you!

You see, at sixteen, I heard God's calling on my life to teach, and I listened. I knew my purpose in life was to make a difference in the lives of children. I had no idea the impact or the reach I would eventually make, all I knew was that I had to be obedient to the calling.

**

Lesson 9: Obedience

Obedience is the very best way to show that you believe, doing exactly what the Lord commands, and doing it happily!

O-B-D-E-I-E-N-C-E

Obedience is the very best way to show that you believe!

43

My grandmother used to sing that song to me at a very young age, and your Nana sings it to you all the time. There are so many things I would not have obtained in my life had I not been obedient to others as well as to my purpose.

Defiance is the opposite of obedience, and there are times when I worry so much about you because I see a propensity to defy authority in you, but obedience prepares us for life.

We have to work to eat, pay bills to live, follow rules to stay out of trouble, and an inability to be obedient can set you on a course to problems later on in your life. We all have to be obedient and answer to someone throughout our lives.

**

As you grew older, I had to talk to you as if you were much mature than you were. We were on our own from the time you were three months old because of your father's military service. While I gave up my military career when we decided to have you, his service continued through retirement. I knew that I could not leave you and did not want to go a day without seeing you.

I believe that the practice of not speaking to you in "baby talk" allowed you to expand your foundation of knowledge. I needed you to understand that, while I am your mother, in order to make it, we needed to work together.

It was rough being a geographically single mom, moving back home, and trying to figure out what I was doing. Thank God we had Nana to help us since we moved with her after your great grandmother passed away. I know that having us there helped her with the devastating loss of her mother as much as it helped us deal with being on our own.

In your eyes, I could see God's promises, and I wanted
nothing more than to work as hard as I could to make sure
that we provided you with opportunities that we never had. I
did not want you to endure the pain that we went through. I
never wanted you to go to bed hungry; however, I want you to
know that the struggle is what made us become the well-
rounded people we grew into. *Without a struggle, there can
be no progress* – Frederick Douglass

Moving to Germany with you and your father was one of the most
difficult things I had to do. You were 9 months old – still a baby –
and had no idea that we were leaving everyone we knew to go and
live in another country. We had just endured a six month
separation based on the military's rules for how often families
could move within a year. Suitcase life was no way to live with a
baby, but we played the cards we were dealt and made the most out
of the separation.

**

Lesson 10: Bitter vs. Better

You have a choice to be better or bitter about a situation – always
choose to be better. If I could, I would make sure that every day
you are on this planet, your days are filled with joy; however, I
know that on a daily basis, people and situations can arise that can
alter our very being and throw our lives into a tailspin. You have a
choice though. You can choose to look at these situations and
whine and complain, or you can choose to look at them as life's
teachable moments. Instead of asking yourself *why is this
happening to me*? ask yourself *why is this happening **for** me*?

I want you to remember that nothing happens by happenstance or
circumstance, but that everything that happens has already been
preordained for your life. There is no reason to be surprised or

45

upset when life happens to us because it will happen. We just have to choose to let these lessons teach us to become better and not allow us to become bitter.

I speak from experience as I think about when your father deployed for 15 months to Iraq. Right before he left, I enrolled in another set of classes to complete my Bachelor's degree in English. I would not be honest with you if I did not tell you that I was scared. So many soldiers had gone and never come back to their families. I suppressed my fear and focused on the task of being your mother – you were now one years old.

**

Lesson 11: Always ask for help when you need it

With your father gone, I needed support to keep a full-time job and be a full time student. I was so blessed to have real friends who I consider to be family to this day. They would come by and watch you just so I could do my assignments, or pick you up so that I could get rest. They even brought us food and came by the hospital when you almost died. Yes, you almost died.

Your dad had only been gone for about two weeks when you got sick. I kept taking you to the doctor's office because, no matter what they gave you, you simply would not get well.

Your daycare called me for the second time in a row within the same week telling me that your fever was up to 102, and I needed to come and pick you up for the day. I took you straight to the clinic for the fourth time in two weeks and was told that you had an ear infection, to give you some Motrin, and let you rest.

I knew something more was going on than just an infection. You were so lethargic, and the joy that was always so present in your face was gone. Instead of driving home as I was instructed, I drove you straight to the Emergency Room.

The doctor who took your vitals diagnosed you with pneumonia. Your lungs were full of fluid; you needed emergency breathing treatments, antibiotics, fluids, and an IV started immediately.

"If you would have taken her home, she would not have survived the night." I will never forget his words.

You had to spend two weeks in the hospital. Thankfully the people who had become like family came and supported us throughout the ordeal. I got to talk to your dad to let him know what happened and that we were okay. I can only imagine the feeling he felt as he was so far away and unable to be there for you.

 Many nights, I would cry thinking about what would have happened if I listened to the people who were supposed to be the "experts" – God had His hand on you then, and He still has His hand on you now!

Always listen to the still small voice on the inside of you. That is the spirit of discernment, and it gives you an ability to judge people and situations well. Whenever I hear that voice, and I wonder if I should listen to it or not, I think about almost losing you. Do not deny that voice.

**

In your formative years, your father's service had him gone so much that you actually believed that he lived in the computer, as that was the only way you could see him. It was both adorable and painful at the same time. It was 2007, and the violence of the war was at its peak.

We visited SFC Johnson's house after learning he was the first in your daddy's unit to be killed in action. I did not know what to say. I felt so guilty because I was so very sad, but relieved that your father was alive. As we knocked on the door, I squeezed your hand. The door creaked open,

"My daddy is in heaven," his youngest son said to us. I thought, *this was a mistake, we should not have come here*, but Mrs. Johnson welcomed us in before I could retreat.

I choked back tears as I hugged her.

"What am I supposed to do now?" She asked me in between her sobs.

"I am so sorry, so, so, sorry." I said as I handed her a card.

What do you say – what can you give to someone who lost the love of their life?

We left. You do not remember this I am sure. You were only two years old.

One night, our doorbell rang at 10:30 pm. Within my circle of friends, we agreed that we would never come to each other's houses unannounced. We knew that a knock on the door could mean someone was coming to tell you that your husband had been killed in action, missing in action, or taken as a prisoner of war. I had not received a phone call. For a moment, I stopped breathing.

They're here to tell me he is gone. I thought to myself. *How can I live without him? How can I go on to take care of my baby?* All these thoughts ran through my head as I swallowed hard to try to get rid of the lump in my throat. I felt sick to my stomach. It was the longest walk to the door. As I twisted the doorknob, I could no longer contain my emotions and burst into tears.

It was only Mr. Alley from my job at the high school telling me something about a practice alert.

"Are you okay?" he asked me.

"You can't do that! You can't come to my house without calling first. You can't...you can't..." I said as I slammed the door in his face simultaneously full of anger and relief. I collapsed to the floor and stayed there sobbing and thanking God that your dad was still alive.

I know it was hard for your father to be away from us each and every day that he was in that war because it was him on the front lines, but we were in our own battle too. We served too.

We watched uniformed service members driving to houses to notify loved ones that their soldier was not coming back. We felt every loss. Our military community mourned together each time we lost a service member.

Each time we did not hear from your father, I knew that it meant that someone had been hurt or killed, and all I could do was pray that it was not him.

One time, when we were on the phone, I heard a loud noise, a gunshot, and dad said,

"I gotta go...I gotta go!" and abruptly hung up the phone.

When I did not hear from him for a day, I spent it worried, knowing something really bad had happened. Finally, the phone rang.

"Honey, I can't talk long. Actually, I snuck on the phone. I wanted to tell you I love you. The noise you heard earlier, someone committed suicide in the bathroom. I promise I will never hurt myself here. I love you. I'm okay." He said as he hung up.

I was so relieved, but so full of agony for the solider who, because of the despondency of war, took his own life.

The most painful component of the Iraq war was that it was predicated on a lie. Our President, George W. Bush, told us that Iraq had weapons of mass destruction, but they did not. We should have NEVER invaded Iraq; we should have never went to war!

Unfortunately, we were there – daddy was there, our friends were there, dealing with the aftermath of a lie. There are still soldiers in Iraq, and, to this day, President Bush has never apologized for the reckless and senseless choice to send hundreds of thousands of our troops in harm's way and caused hundreds of thousands of Iraqi civilians to lose their lives from that war.

I tell you all of this in an effort for you to understand the ugliness of war, and the damage a lie can do.

**

Lesson 12: Your word is your bond.

Always be able to stand on the word of truth, and be a person of your word. Lies can kill, but the truth sets us free. Also, when you make a mistake, be willing to accept the consequences of that mistake and take ownership. To have integrity means to have strong moral values and to be honest. In this world we live in today, with so many people lying and not displaying decent morals, I know it will be difficult for you to maintain your uprightness, but you must do so. You have to remain who you are at your core – a person who is honest, keeps your word, and does the right thing.

**

I knew I was beyond ready for your father to come home after we were on a call, and I actually heard him come under mortar attack.

"BOOM! BOOM!" I heard on the other end of the phone.

"What is that? What's happening?"

"Mortar fire – we are under mortar fire…," I heard him say as the sirens started to shrill in the background. Then, the phone cut off, and all I could hear was the dial tone. Silence.

I felt the air leave my body as if I was deflated in that millisecond. I was in the middle of the store on my cell phone during the phone call, but I felt alone in the world in that moment although life was moving all around me. People were living, going about their day, and your dad was fighting. I wanted to scream – *We are at war! People are in danger!* But I remained quiet and resolute until I got to my car. Once I got in my car, I sat there and cried, screamed, and beat the steering wheel for several minutes before going to pick you up from daycare.

Just writing about it now – I have to pause, gather myself, and fight back tears. To know that he was in danger in the middle of Baghdad, Iraq and have our phone conversation cut off was a fear that is difficult to place into words. I was helpless to assist and had to wait until the next phone call to know if everything was alright – to know if he survived it.

When your great-grandfather died while daddy was in Iraq, SGT Vrooman was so helpful while he was in charge of taking care of the families back in Germany. His wife and two little babies were so precious. I think fondly on the company Halloween party that we all attended as you played with his children.

It was a painful time because I could not go home to be with my family. With work and school, I just could not leave, but SGT Vrooman came by to check on us and made sure that we were okay since we were not able to be with our loved ones.

After 12 months in Iraq, your dad finally got a chance to come home on Rest and Relaxation (R&R) for a visit. You were so angry with us for going away for a few days when he returned. I can only imagine what your two year old mind must have been thinking.

My daddy is back. He lives in the computer and has been gone almost my whole life. He came back and now he took my mommy.

When we got back to pick you up, you cried and ran to embrace us, but then you scrunched up your eyebrows, folded your arms, and stopped speaking to us for two days. I think back to my hurt and sorrow during that time at your response to us and can only imagine the fear you must have endured but were unable to articulate.

We learned the day we were coming to get you that SGT Vrooman, who had only been in Iraq for 30 days, was killed in action.

As tears stain these pages as I write, I still mourn his death – I still feel the guilt that someone's husband and father will never get to see their children grow up. It hurts as much in today as it did in 2008. Knowing that your dad had to go back for three more months was even more painful in light of SGT Vrooman's death.

A unit daddy was assigned to, but got moved from right before his deployment to Iraq, had seven soldiers walk into a booby trapped house. When the bomb detonated, all seven of them died. That could have been your dad, but God spared his life. War is ugly – it takes no less than everything from everyone involved. There are both physical scars and there are scars that you cannot see.

I often wish you could have gotten to know your father before Iraq.
Lately, he has been more of himself as he was before the war, but
we lost a part of him there. A piece of your father died in Iraq.

When your father came back home in November, he had to go
through reintegration prior to fully coming back home. I feel like
we needed to go through it too. Reintegration was supposed to
create a smoother transition back into family life for the soldiers.
After living each day on high alert, coming home proved to be
difficult for many members of the armed forces.

When many of the people came back home from Iraq from daddy's
unit, we noticed that a lot of them ended up getting a divorce. The
divorce rate in the military during Iraq and Afghanistan increased
by 42% (Oleszczuk, 2012). This is a part of the ugliness of war
that I told you about. It is not natural to be apart for a long period
of time as a family.

I had no idea what we were in store for, but I knew your dad
arrived back home very withdrawn, sad, and unable to sleep. I did
not know how to get him back to his old self. I know it is difficult
to understand how someone could be unhappy to be out of harm's
way, but dad was not experiencing these feelings alone. So many
people were returning with post-traumatic stress disorder.

I believe that for a period of time, your dad had survivor's remorse.
I know that he was thankful to be alive, but at the same time, he
felt guilty about the friends he lost. The worse part was that I could
not relate, so he had no outlet to share his feelings of guilt,
confusion, and depression.

After your dad's return, we would argue over simple things such as
picking up the mail. Yes, picking up the mail seems like something
most couples would never fight about, but when you had been
responsible for everything for 15 months, it can be hard to release

some of those responsibilities back to your partner.

To be honest with you, I had lived so much for you and your father prior to his deployment, that I had become unrecognizable to myself. When he left, I had to learn how to be dependent on myself. I did not even know how to cut the grass, was not accustomed to taking out the trash, or assembling things on my own because he did so much. While I missed him very much, learning who I was independent of being your mother and his wife was liberating.

**

Lesson 13: Always be true to yourself and never lose yourself in anything or anyone. I worry so much about you staying true to your core. Daddy tells you every morning to be who you are and not who you are not. So many things will come into your life to distract you from who God called you to be, but always remember that you were fearfully and wonderfully made. People who love you will love you for you – always stay true to you.

**

Doing all those things while your father was gone allowed me to get back to the essence of who I was. So something as simple as going to pick up the mail was something that I did not want to give up. Your dad did not understand this, and for him, he simply wanted to get back to the life he left behind. The life that seemed to move forward in his absence.

I did not understand that my desire for independence was making him feel like we did not need him, and those feelings were coupled with the inner conflict he was fighting about his emotions about the war he had just come home from.

During the time he was gone, the 2008 Presidential election was in full swing. It was truly a historic one too! When it first began, I thought we were about to see the first woman elected to office. Hillary Clinton was running a strong race, but I remember being at my friend's house and seeing that Senator Obama was announcing his candidacy.

As you were running around playing, one of her associates, who happened to be at her house, a white woman, said, "America will NEVER elect a Black president."

I wrinkled up my eyebrows at her ignorant words and said, "I think he is going to win."

I started to take notice of Senator Obama four years earlier in 2004 while I was still serving in the Army. He was speaking at the Democratic National Convention on behalf of the Democratic nominee Senator John Kerry.

I will never forget his words as I laid in my bed at Fort Campbell, KY dealing with the possibility of deploying to Iraq because of the lies perpetuated by the Bush administration. Your father and I were living in two different places because the Army would not station us together.

I was especially interested in politics, as who sat in the office had a direct impact on mine and your father's lives as soldiers in the United States Army.

The first time I heard Barack Obama's voice, I was drawn to his stature, stage presence, and charisma. Senator Obama spoke about being the son of an immigrant from Kenya and a white woman from Kansas. He talked about how his name meant "blessed". As parents, we choose to give you both names with meaning. Your name's mean "God has heard" and "Beautiful".

55

If I Could   Kelisa J. Wing

His words touched my heart in my bedroom in 2004, and he caused me to believe that America could and would be better.

"This is not a red America or a blue America, but it is the United States of America," (Obama, 2004).

Never in my lifetime had a politician made me feel so hopeful about what America could be, so when I saw Senator Obama was running for President, I could not have been more excited. Although I knew that it was a longshot, I still wanted to believe that America could look beyond his skin color, place country over politics, and elect this man who was the best choice for the nation.

Years prior to his speech, Senator Obama wrote a beautiful story called *Dreams of My Father* where he dove even deeper into what brought his father from Kenya to America and what led him on a journey to find the father he never knew.

I was reading *The Audacity of Hope* around the time when he announced his presidency, and that is the best way I can explain the feeling we as Americans were feeling, buoyant.

During this time we were still living in Germany. For the first time, I donated to a political campaign and signed up to assist in any way possible. Since we were living overseas, I could not go canvassing or knocking on doors, so I made phone calls, donated, and told as many people as I could about Senator Obama and why he should lead our country. I wasn't going to let the fact that I was not in the country stop my activism. Because of his run, I stopped placing limitations on myself. I never believed a Black man or woman could be president, but I did with him.

When he secured the nomination, it was a huge accomplishment that no person of color had achieved. It is difficult to place into words the feeling we had at the time, especially reflecting on it now, as we have strayed so far away from that feeling.

As Senator Obama's book stated, we had the audacity to hope. We dared to believe that we deserved to run the country that our ancestors built. "Yes we can," was our rallying cry.

Not long after your father came back from Iraq, it was election night and time to see if Senator Obama would become President Obama.

We stayed up until 3:00 am to see if history would be made. We allowed you to stay up with us. You did not quite understand what was happening. "Bo-rock and Chelle Obama," you affectionately called them at the tender age of two. You cannot begin to imagine how elated I felt for you to see images of a Black family on the television that were authentic, loving, and positive.

"Did Bo-rock win mommy?," you asked me.

"We don't really know yet." I said to you as you curled up in my lap.

After hours of intense waiting, Wolf Blitzer announced, "We can now project that Barack Obama will be our 44th President."

Tears streamed down my face. I laughed, sobbed, hugged you and your father, and thanked God.

"Why are you crying mommy?"

"Because he did it – we did it!"

For you, a toddler, that was not a large accomplishment. Before your 3rd birthday, we had a Black president. For all you knew, this was as it always had been. However, for me, someone who was told to go back to Africa, who was called a nigger, who felt like the "least of these", this was a moment I would never forget.

We watched him, Michelle, Sasha, and Malia take the stage. This beautiful, radiant, Black family. You have to understand the role that the government played in destroying Black men and the ripple effect that led to the demise of Black families in the 1980s. The root cause of this demise can be traced back to slavery and separating fathers and mothers, sons and daughters, and yet, through it all, here we were watching this Black man accept and acknowledge the results of the election.

This election had many firsts and many stories that will be told for generations. But one that's on my mind tonight's about a woman who cast her ballot in Atlanta. She's a lot like the millions of others who stood in line to make their voice heard in this election except for one thing: Ann Nixon Cooper is 106 years old.

She was born just a generation past slavery; a time when there were no cars on the road or planes in the sky; when someone like her couldn't vote for two reasons -- because she was a woman and because of the color of her skin.

And tonight, I think about all that she's seen throughout her century in America [...]: Yes we can.

She was there for the buses in Montgomery, the hoses in Birmingham, a bridge in Selma, and a preacher from Atlanta who told a people that "We Shall Overcome." Yes we can. [...]

And this year, in this election, she touched her finger to a screen, and cast her vote, because after 106 years in America, through the best of times and the darkest of hours, she knows how America can change.

Yes we can. (Obama, 2008)

As I reminisce on this beautiful time in our history, as our nation is now embroiled in the throngs of an Impeachment hearing, I cannot help but to smile and wipe away a tear at the same time thinking about how much we have fallen since then.

That night, I tucked you into your bed feeling like your future was bright and I was happy about the direction our country was heading.

**

Lesson 14: Joy vs. Happiness: Endeavor to have joy because happiness can be fleeting. I believe that when we say we are happy, it is because something is "happening", but when you have joy, you understand that joy is not based on something or someone. You have to have joy in your heart during good times and bad times. Happiness can be short-lived, so hold tight to joy.

**

Watching you develop into your own personality was a delight! I was so amazed at how well you played by yourself and kept yourself entertained. Most of our friends' children were much older than you, so you acted more mature than you were.

I always wanted to expose you to as many things as possible so that you could discover your niche. We started you in gymnastics and Girl Scouts. Then we took you to ballet, and, to our surprise, you were very good at it. Unfortunately, due to your behavior, we pulled you out of it right before your recital, and you never danced again.

I hope that you remember that obedience is always better than sacrifice. I don't know who was more hurt about the recital, you or me, but we had to show you that for every action, there is a reaction and your behavior has consequences.

You stuck with Girl Scouts because we liked the fact that it allowed you to give back to the community through service. I believe that the very reason we are here us to serve others.

Living in Germany, we were shielded from the struggles that were going on in the world. On a visit home one year, I caught wind of a story about a 7 year old girl who was killed by law enforcement in Detroit (Washington, 2019).

After about a year, you began to start to ask for a brother or a sister. I was not trying to hear that because I was still traumatized from all we went through with your birth. You were five years old.

"Mommy, can we pray?"

Of course," I said to you as I tucked you in bed.

"Dear God, please give me a brother or sister so that I can love them and they can love me. In Jesus' name. Amen."

You were laying it on thick, and you prayed that prayer every night for several months.

While watching you play alone, your dad began to think about how neither one of us grew up without siblings, and it wasn't fair for you to grow up without a sibling in the house. Yes, you have an older brother, but due to complicated circumstances, he wasn't able to be around much. We tried to make our blended family work – we really did, but it seemed like no matter what we did, it never worked out well.

As a child who wanted to have my father in my life, it broke my heart to watch your dad want to be in your brother's life and have to face so much adversity.

**

Lesson 15: "The ultimate measure of a man is not where he stands in moments of comfort and convenience, but where he stands at times of challenge and controversy" – Martin Luther King, Jr.

I want you to know that in life, just because you do what is right, it does not mean others will. That will not only frustrate you, but it will confuse you as well. Do not let it. With the situation with your older brother, I would pray about, fast about it, cry about it, but nothing seemed to help. All I could do was remain kind, resolute, loving, and trust God to do the rest. What I did not do was allow the situation to make my heart turn cold. In the face of adversity, always strive to remain in the center of God's love and display mercy and grace. Your character should never be changed in hard times. Tough times do not last long but tough people do.

**

When your dad shared his thoughts with me, I agreed that we should try to give you a sibling.

Part III: Peace that Surpasses All Understanding

Part III: Peace the Surpasses All Understanding

When we started trying to have you, we thought it would be just as easy as when we tried to have your sister. Back then, it was as simple as saying *let's try to have a baby*, and two weeks later, we were pregnant.

A few years prior to us trying to conceive you, I learned that I was in early ovarian failure. At the time, it didn't matter much to me because your father and I decided that we weren't going to have any more children.

After two months of trying for a baby, I remembered my earlier diagnosis and realized it was not going to be so easy to conceive. As each month passed by, I found myself agonizing as to why I wasn't getting pregnant.

I started to buy fertility kits so that I would know if I was ovulating or not. What should have been a beautiful experience became like a second job with me wanting so desperately to get pregnant. After nine months, I believed that it would never happen, but faith is the substance of things hoped for and the evidence of things not seen (Hebrews 11:1).

On a whim, I decided to take a pregnancy test although I was

64

almost certain that it was not going to bring me the results I so desperately sought.

As I sat on the bathroom floor waiting to be disappointed, I saw a plus sign. I frantically scoured through the trash can to retrieve the box that I had thrown away to see what sign I should see.

Plus means pregnant minus means not pregnant.

I refused to allow myself to get excited just in case it was a false positive. I took another test – plus again!

I began to cry and thank God that He answered our prayers once again! I did not take the ability to carry life lightly, especially when so many women and men struggle with infertility.

Two years before your sister was born, a scare with cancer caused me to have to undergo surgery. I was told by that doctor that I might not be able to carry a child, so the fact that I had her and was able to get pregnant again was nothing short of a miracle and an assuredness that God does answer prayers.

The next day, I went to my doctor's office for another pregnancy test – just to be sure. She confirmed that I was indeed pregnant and placed my due date for late December or early January.

I was very elated, but under a lot of stress during this time of my life. I had just finished my Master's degree, and the stress of trying to conceive was starting to impact my health as well as mine and your father's relationship.

I could not quite put my finger on it, but I sensed that something was wrong with me health wise. A few days after learning that I was pregnant, your sister, father, and I made the long drive to Heidelberg, Germany for my graduation. It was surreal to finally be finished with school. I was so proud to have your sister watch me accomplish such a milestone. I hoped to be a positive influence in your lives by demonstrating perseverance to pursue my education.

We got back home from Heidelberg just in time to go to church. I was feeling so hopeful for our family's future and the future of my unborn child. After church, your sister had me in her room having a "tea party" although I was unusually tired. I remember it vividly, I had on my comfortable pajamas, bathrobe, and house slippers.

I had not yet told your sister that I was pregnant. I knew she would be jubilant at the news. All of a sudden, I felt a sharp pain in my stomach.

I went to the bathroom, as I felt a gush of blood rush down my leg.

"Lord, please protect my baby," I prayed as I tried to clean myself up.

"Something is wrong," I told you father. They took me to the hospital.

"What's wrong mommy?" Your sister asked me.

"Nothing baby," I reassured her.

The doctor's had me to lie down as they drew blood and did an ultrasound.

"I'm not seeing anything," the doctor said, "Let's see what the bloodwork gives us.

As I waited, I continued to pray. I asked God to protect our family. I asked God to protect my baby. I asked God to show favor to us, and to make sure that my baby was okay.

We then waited and waited.

The doctor arrived with a desolate look in her eyes.

"I'm so sorry to tell you that based on your HCG levels, it appears that you are having a miscarriage. The low level of HCG indicates that your body is in the early stages of a miscarriage and is rejecting ."

Miscarriage, me? I couldn't comprehend. I could not understand.

"Is there anything we can do," Your father frantically asked as he squeezed my hand.

"No, unfortunately not. This is much more common than you would think. Sometimes the body will reject a pregnancy if something is wrong. We will never know. All you can do is go home and wait," The doctor said.

Rejecting that word stung. Why would my body reject something so beautiful?

We left the hospital in silence and drove home. The next day, your father and I went to speak with our pastors to share the news and prayed with them for a different outcome.

Your father so desperately wanted everything to work out, but I believed with each passing moment that I was losing the baby.

"If I am losing my baby, I just want to ask God to give me the peace that surpasses all understanding," I said to him and our spiritual leaders.

I did not need to know why – I just wanted to be okay with it.

**

Lesson 16: Just because you want something, does not always mean you are going to get it. We can pray, beg, and plead our way out of a situation; however, sometimes it is not God's plan to get us out of the situation. He may have a bigger plan for our lives that we cannot comprehend. Isaiah 55:8-9 says,

8 "For My thoughts are not your thoughts,
Nor are your ways My ways," says the Lord.
⁹⁹ "For as the heavens are higher than the earth,
So are My ways higher than your ways,
And My thoughts than your thoughts."

What the Lord is reminding us, is that we do not know what His plan is for our lives, but we should understand that ultimately, it is vital that His will be done. Denying your will can be painful, but it is necessary for navigating through life. Just know that all things are working together for your good in the end.

**

For the next few days, I continued to work and take care of your sister, as well as mourn the loss of the baby. After the third day, I was no longer pregnant – my child was gone.

We took a family trip, and reconnected as a family unit in Spain. Beauty and serenity was all around us, and we basked in the moment of escaping the trauma of what had occurred.

I decided I would no longer labor over having a baby. If it was meant to happen, if it was a part of God's plan, it would happen. Once I came to that realization, I came to a place of complete peace.

About four weeks after the loss of your unborn brother or sister, I wondered why I had not gone through the natural cycle a woman should experience. On a whim, I thought, maybe I should take a pregnancy test.

I was not surprised that the test indicated that I was pregnant because I assumed I still had the HCG hormone in my body. I waited a few days before going to the hospital to get a blood test because I really did not believe that I was truly "pregnant".

We had to wait a while to get the results back from the blood test.

"It is positive," the doctor said.

"Is that just a trace of the HCG from the miscarriage?" I asked.

"No, the level of HCG in your blood is very high. When you were experiencing your miscarriage, your level of HCG was lower than where it is now. This is a new pregnancy."

With tears streaming down my face, I began to thank God right there in the doctor's office.

"For many people, it can take about 3 months to conceive again, so it is uncanny for you to be pregnant so fast. Congratulations to you," the doctor said as he gently placed his hand on my shoulder.

My due date was set in February, only about six weeks after your brother or sister would have been born.

Your father and I understood this time around how fragile life could be. I never thought that I would lose a baby. We do not often speak about such things as we never imagined that such a loss could be our experience. We were both overjoyed with the thought of being with child, but we were hesitant to share this news with anyone.

A few weeks later, I was tasked to go to a training for work with a colleague a few hours away from home. As the morning progressed along, I sat quietly thinking about the life that was inside of me when all of a sudden the sharp pain I felt when I was losing my baby shot through my stomach.

I quickly went to the restroom to find that I was bleeding.

"No, no, no…God I cannot endure this again. Please Jesus, protect my baby. No…," I pleaded with God.

I wiped away tears as I exited the restroom. I pulled my colleague to the side and explained to him that I needed to leave, as he was my ride.

"I, we, have to go. I need to get to the hospital. I am pregnant, but I think I…my baby…something is wrong."

He was a God-fearing man, and he prayed for me right there. We left right away and made the long 2 hour drive to the hospital.

It was the longest ride of my life.

I cried and prayed the entire way.

Lord, I asked you for the peace that surpasses all understanding for the loss of my last baby, but Lord please don't allow this to happen again. I don't know if I could survive this. I know that I have come to you many times before with many requests, but God please hear my heart's desire and save my baby.

By the time I got to the hospital, I was bleeding heavily, and although I trusted the Lord, I believed in my heart, I was going to lose my child – for a second time.

Your dad was waiting at the hospital for me, and I could see the concern on his face. He suffered the loss of the baby too, and although it was happening in my body, we mourned together.

The doctor decided to do a blood test, and again, we had to wait a while for the results.

We quietly held hands and waited. I knew that I needed to find a quiet place where I could be alone with God, so I found the only place I could, which was the restroom.

As soon as I locked the door behind me, I fell to my knees and began to sob. I felt like I had cried with everything I had inside of me. I began to shake and gasp for air.

Please don't allow this – please Lord, please. I would not survive this loss. I don't know what is going on, but I am begging you – let me have this baby.

While I was crying, I was petitioning the Lord to have mercy on me and to show favor on us. I held my stomach because I was crying so hard that it began to hurt. I cried until I had nothing in me. In that moment, it felt as if the walls fell from around me. I no longer was in the restroom, but I was sitting in the presence of the Lord lying flat on my face at His feet. I suddenly felt a peace and a warmth all over my body.

**

Lesson 17: Trust in the Lord with all your heart and lean not to your own understanding. You have to remember that God is working things out for you, so trust Him for the results that are best for you. The key is to trust Him.

**

I sat up on the cold bathroom floor, realizing my location once again. I straightened myself out and went out of the restroom back to the waiting area.

Not long after, the doctor showed up,

"We have your results. Your HCG levels have tripled since you were last here."

"What does that mean?," I asked.

"It means that your baby is doing fine. Let's do an ultrasound."

Your father and I embraced, and were thankful, but still very concerned.

As I got the ultrasound done, the doctor showed me where you were.

"There's the baby right there, and over here, that is where the blood is coming from. We are not sure why you are bleeding and we are not sure when or if the bleeding will stop," he explained.

"Is the baby going to be alright?," We both asked.

"We are not sure if this is going to be a viable pregnancy, so we would like see you weekly."

The word viable was one that reverberated in my mind. I was told that I would be classified as a high risk pregnancy and was placed on bed rest for the next few weeks.

All of this was happening at the end of the school year. I student taught 12th grade that year and missed the graduation. I sent cards to my seniors telling them I wished I could be there, and remained in bed while your dad attended in my stead.

We continued to keep my pregnancy a secret deciding it would be best to wait until I was in the 3rd trimester before we shared the news with anyone outside of our church leaders. All the while, I continued to bleed, and my worry for you continued to grow with each day. Each doctor's visit we were reassured that you were alright, but they still had no answer as to why I was bleeding.

Kelisa Wing   If I Could

Some nights, I would dream I lost you, only to wake up abruptly from my sleep and grab my growing belly. At my weekly checkups, I was afraid that I would not hear your heartbeat.

I shared my fears with my pastor's wife.

"Each day, I want you to place your hand over your stomach and recite Jeremiah 1:5 to your baby."

Jeremiah 1:5 Before I formed you in the womb I knew you; Before you were born I sanctified you; I ordained you a prophet to the nations.

After weeks of remaining in bed, I decided that I could no longer live in fear about losing you. I understood that if it was God's will for you to be here, you would be here and remaining in fear or in the bed was not going to change that fact.

I went back to work and continued to trust the Lord, go to my weekly appointments, and speak that scripture to you. I was not interested in your gender this time around, all I wanted was to have a healthy baby; however, we soon learned you were a boy. I was happy, but ultimately, I just wanted you to be okay.

Due to the traumatic nature of your sister's birth, I was very anxious about what would happen during your delivery. My doctor was very understanding. He saw me through the miscarriage, my pregnancy, and he would be performing my delivery via cesarean. He promised me he would not do any procedures until he was absolutely certain that I was medically ready unlike the doctor I dealt with when having your sister.

The day of your birth felt very different than when I had your sister. I was in such a serene place because I was a bit more prepared for what was about to happen. This time, I knew I was

73

going to be having surgery, and I was given the option to be put to sleep or partially awake.

"I want to see him," I said to the doctor explaining why I did not want to be put to sleep.

When I was wheeled into the operating room this time, Dr. Sanjay squeezed my arm and said,

"Everything is going to be fine. I won't do anything until I am absolutely sure that you are numb."

I felt so much better knowing that he was empathetic to my needs in that moment.

"Do you feel that?" He asked me.

"Feel what?" I asked feeling nice and loopy.

"You are ready."

He proceeded to perform the cesarean, explaining to your father and I everything that was happening along the way. Then, I heard you cry.

Until that very moment, at around 9:30 am February 7th, I was not sure throughout my entire pregnancy if I would hear you cry, if I would meet you in person, if God would see fit for me to be your mother in this lifetime, but when I heard you cry – it was like the first time I saw a butterfly, the first time I saw the autumn leaves changing from green to a warm orange, the first time I smelled the crisp winter air, and it was the most beautiful sound I had heard. It is hard to explain my feelings. Yes, I trusted God, but I placed my complete trust in Him understanding that I could not control anything about what could happen although I so desperately wanted to have you.

They laid you on my chest briefly, then told me that they had to take you out to do vitals on you. My blood pressure dropped so low that I began to shake profusely, and they had to perform several medical procedures to bring it back up.

After a long morning, we were all reunited with everyone doing well.

Your sister was so excited to meet you that afternoon. As she held you, she marveled at how small you were. She giggled as she reminded us that she was the reason you were here because she "asked" for you. I sat back in my hospital bed admiring you both wrapped up in the moment, not thinking about the outside world, forgetting about all the strife and only focusing on our family, our love, and our fleeting security.

19 days after your birth, Trayvon Martin was murdered, and I was woke to the fact that I now had a son – a Black son.

Part IV: Thick Skin and a Tender Heart

Part IV: Thick Skin and a Tender Heart

I am pleased God made my skin Black. I wish He had made it thicker – Curt Flood

Apostle Lyndon Townsend often talks about the need for us as believers to have thick skin and a tender heart. In this life, we will be hurt, talked about, lied on, and see all types of things that are unjust; however, we have to continue to love others – hence the tender heart. Having a hard heart towards others will cause us to reciprocate the behavior that they have bestowed upon us and others.

Our skin must remain thick in order to deal with this world. Having thick skin allows our feelings to not be easily hurt by others. I hope as you both grow up, you have thick skin and a tender heart in all matters.

**

Lesson 18: Don't try to fit in when you were made to stand out. When I was younger, I would often feel hurt when I did not get invited to certain events or when I was not friended by someone I deemed "popular". Having thick skin means that you are not easily offended. I hope that you will not try hard to fit in when you were made to stand out from the crowd. I often think about how grateful I am not to be in certain circles. Always remember that you will not be accepted by everyone, and that is okay. Those who are for you will be for you, and those who are not will not – you have to accept it, continue to love, and move on.

**

Being a Black person in America means being perceived as a threat. It is difficult not to personalize this, as it is happening personally to you, but you have to understand that the issue is not with you, but with the person who chooses to see things from that perspective.

Now raising a Black boy, the murder of Trayvon Martin was one that caught my attention on the news. You spent most of your time in my arms sleeping in the first few weeks of your life while I was on maternity leave.

It initially appeared that the murderer would not be charged with a crime at all, which was like being victimized all over again for Trayvon's family.

Because we lived in Germany, we were a bit detached from the 24 news cycle that is pervasive in the states; however, his murder was reported internationally, so it was difficult to ignore.

Trayvon's death hit different for me. A toy cop, the neighborhood watch, felt that he could assume the role of a police officer and take his life because, in his mind, Trayvon did not belong.

We were in the midst of moving back to the states in July, and I paid close attention to what was happening in the case.

In November 2012, Jordan Davis was murdered by a white man in Florida who said that he felt threatened because Jordan's music was playing too loudly from the car.

I could not help but think how many times as a young soldier I played my music very loudly from my car at a gas station. What would have happened to me if someone "felt threatened" by the music I chose to listen to loudly as a carefree 20 year old. This man was protected by the stand your ground law for a short time; however, he was found guilty and sentenced to life in prison.

It seemed like these occurrences were getting out of hand and happening so often that we were starting to wonder when it would happen again.

Although it was vindication for Jordan's murderer to be found guilty when so many others were not, it did not take away the pain of the loss of yet another Black boy, a child, someone's baby.

Unfortunately, for Trayvon, justice was elusive. I felt that people were becoming more emboldened to do harm to people of color because others were getting away with these crimes.

I remember watching Trayvon's trial with you on my hip most days. I would watch the television in anger and confusion. I could not understand why they were vilifying this boy who was only a child.

I would listen to the trial and look at you, wondering about the future and hoping that this time, for Trayvon, would be different. His killer was found not guilty. It felt unfair, unjust, and all too familiar.

We were living in the South during this time, and for all of the firmly held beliefs I heard about living there and how people were racist, I came to realize that the Northeast and the Midwest were much more cruel and racist than this new place we called home.

A few years after Jordan Davis and Trayvon Martin were killed, Michael Brown was gunned down, another unarmed Black teen shot and killed for no reason.

I continued to try to protect you guys from the news and would often shut off the TV so that you would not be aware of the world out there that posed such a danger to people who looked like us.

We were living in a nice home, had nice jobs, and worked hard to give you the things we did not have, but as we saw all too often, we were still who we were no matter what we achieved in life. In the streets, anything could happen to us if a police officer decided to take our life, and they would find an excuse to justify it.

November 2014, Tamir Rice, a 12 year old boy, was murdered for playing with a toy gun. No warning, no command, just a gunshot and the loss of his life.

 I could not help but think about the constant policing I endured in the inner city as a child around the same age as Tamir. We had police officers on bikes, horses, on foot, in patrol cars, you name it, there were police everywhere. There were police in my school along with metal detectors and the threat of going to the police station if you messed up and did something that normally would land a child in the principal's office.

This constant policing led to a distrust on both sides; to them, we were something to be controlled or handled, and to us, they were constantly watching us waiting for us to mess up so that they could either take our freedom or our lives.

One summer evening, my stepbrothers and I were playing with a neon green toy gun in the alley when an officer approached us,

"You better put that gun down. We could mistake it for a real one and shoot you," He said in a joking manner; however, the chill that ran down my spine reinforced that this was no joke.

That moment never left me. That he could kill me in my neighborhood, near my house, for playing like every other kid was doing and nothing would happen. All he had to say was that he "feared for his life".

For Michael Brown, although tragic, his murder sparked a movement. Scores of people incorporated the saying: "Hands up Don't Shoot" and soon after, the hashtag #BlackLivesMatter was birthed.

Many other people tried to say that all lives matter should have been what was embraced; however, all majority lives have always mattered, but Black and Brown lives have never mattered as much as others. To truly understand this, it is important to understand that Black people in America during the 400 years we endured in captivity were never viewed as people, but as property. In the same manner that we own cars and houses today, that is how we were viewed.

Dontre Hamilton, Sandra Bland, Walter Scott, Oscar Grant, LaQuan McDonald, Lakia Boyd, John Crawford III, Shawn Bell, Amadou Diallo, Freddie Gray, Johnathan Farrel, Ezell Ford, Dante Parker, Tanisha Anderson, Akai Gurley, Rumain Brisbon, Jerame Reid, Tony Robinson, Phillip White, and Eric Harris were just some of the other people who were murdered between 2014 and 2015 by the very people who were supposed to protect and serve them although there were many more.

I place their names here so that you can know that they lived, loved, dreamed, had hopes, fears, and wonders. They deserved a chance to live a full life – the same way you deserve it too.

By the time Philando Castile was murdered, we were beyond tired. It was as if like there was a blatant disregard for Black and Brown lives. Time and time again we saw someone gunned down only to not be held accountable and continue to be able to live their lives.

Our decision to talk to you both at the pool in Florida was very hard. I worried that you were not old enough to understand, and I wavered between allowing you to remain blissfully ignorant or shockingly woke. We chose the latter.

We could not pretend that your privilege – because you do have a level of privilege – negated the fact that you are Black. It will not keep you from being a threat, educated or not, to some people in society.

You experienced this first hand last year when you were 6 years old. A white student accused you of stealing chips and, although you vehemently denied it, you were interrogated by the school resource officer only for the little boy to discover his chips had fallen to the bottom of his book bag.

Remembering our talk years prior, you came home afraid and shaken up and told me what happened. I did not receive so much as a phone call or notification while you were having your civil rights violated and being treated like a criminal. I did not think you would be questioned by the police at such a young age especially at school but the school-to-prison pipeline is real and knows no bounds.

We know that the ability to protect yourselves will be in your awareness that this is the world in which you are living. It will also require you to have the wherewithal to love others in spite of their ignorance – to have thick skin and a tender heart.

"When they go low, we go high." – Michelle Obama

Part V: Be Great

Part V: Be Great

If you want to be important—wonderful. If you want to be recognized—wonderful. If you want to be great—wonderful. But recognize that he who is greatest among you shall be your servant. That's a new definition of greatness.

And this morning, the thing that I like about it: by giving that definition of greatness, it means that everybody can be great because everybody can serve. You don't have to have a college degree to serve. You don't have to make your subject and your verb agree to serve. You don't have to know about Plato and Aristotle to serve. You don't have to know Einstein's theory of relativity to serve. You don't have to know the second theory of thermodynamics in physics to serve. You only need a heart full of grace, a soul generated by love. And you can be that servant.

- Martin Luther King, Jr. "The Drum Major Effect"

All parents want their children to be leaders and not followers. However, I want you both to understand that leadership is not about being in charge. It is not about a position or a title, but it is about service.

We often talk about Dr. Martin Luther King, Jr. and his *I have a*

Dream speech, but to understand service as leadership, one must study Martin Luther King Jr.'s life and words in their entirety.

In his sermon, "The Drum Major Effect", King compels us that we are not truly great unless we are in the service of others. That service does not require a degree, a license, or credentials, that service simply requires a desire to deny self and to serve others.

To whom much is given, much is required, and you both have been given a lot. Your gifts that you have inside of you were not given for you but for you to share with the world. I want you both to remember that leadership has never been about the position or power, but about leveraging that leadership to provide access for those who benefit from the position and the power that the leadership provides.

As you get older, you may aspire to leadership for a myriad of reasons; however, as the quote acknowledges, some people want to be recognized or known, but the true purpose of leadership is service. As a person who is committed to social justice, I need you to understand that if you have a seat at the table, you have a responsibility to speak power to truth with the truth enveloped in love.

You may not understand why, although we could, we did not send you to the district with the most resources and the highest test scores. We studied the demographics and noticed that you would likely be the only students of color sitting in the classroom, and we did not want that.

Living in New York, I saw firsthand what a lack of diversity could do to you both. For you, baby girl, it caused you to come home confused at the micro and macro aggressions you endured when students would make comments about your natural hair or say ignorant things like,

"Go sit in the chair over there. It's black like you."

You struggled between how to handle those situations when there was no one to discuss it with at your school and how to understand how people who said they were your friends could cut you so deep with their words.

For you, my son, I watched you go from a precocious kindergartner who went from loving school to thinking something was wrong with you and not liking it all. You were keenly aware of the fact that you seemed to get in more trouble for developmentally appropriate behaviors than your peers did. I was shocked to walk through the hallway and see you sitting in a chair away from the group because your teacher felt that you were not sitting still on the carpet. I questioned my own parenting during this time thinking I needed to punish you more to change you to fit into her idea of what a "good" student was. I saw the damage this was doing to you when one night I tucked you into bed and you said,

"I am a bad person mommy."

I decided then that I had to be in the service of you and get you out of this toxic environment by any means necessary. The hardest part was to know that I was an Assistant Principal in your school, and I was powerless to help you.

The teacher refused to meet with me without a full team of people so that we could remedy the situation, and I felt a lack of support from my leadership. I felt like because I was the Assistant Principal, I was not allowed to be your mother and advocate for you. Couple this with the fact that I was one of the only people of color – minus the only teacher of color that I hired – I felt very helpless to support you. I still fought within the confines that I could.

I made moves to advance my career and move on so that you could have a better school experience. There was no way I was going to stay there and watch you be deprecated by a disparate school system that was not set up for you to be treated justly.

I have told you both that during my time in school, I only had two Black teachers and they were both female, one in the fifth grade and the other in seventh grade.

Never seeing myself represented in the teachers who taught me never stopped me from wanting to be an educator. In your life, never lose sight of your dreams and do not let anyone or anything stop you. If people will not let you sit at their table, go make a new table.

Nationally, only 18 percent of teachers are of color. Out of the 18 percent, 7 percent are Black and of that only 2 percent are Black men (NCES, 2012), and we know that teachers of color are good for all students.

Throughout high school, I was the only Black girl in my honors class. In the 11th grade, I was the only camp counselor of color. Back then, it never really registered with me that I was one of the few.

As Black people, we deal with the psychological pressure of double consciousness, described by W.E.B. Dubois as,

[...] a peculiar sensation, this double-consciousness, this sense of always looking at one's self through the eyes of others, of measuring one's soul by the tape of a world that looks on in amused contempt and pity. One ever feels his two-ness, an American, a Negro; two souls, two thoughts, two unreconciled strivings; two warring ideals in one dark body, whose dogged strength alone keeps it from being torn asunder. The history of the

American Negro is the history of this strife- this longing to attain self-conscious manhood, to merge his double self into a better and truer self. In this merging he wishes neither of the older selves to be lost. He does not wish to Africanize America, for America has too much to teach the world and Africa. He wouldn't bleach his Negro blood in a flood of white Americanism, for he knows that Negro blood has a message for the world. He simply wishes to make it possible for a man to be both a Negro and an American without being cursed and spit upon by his fellows, without having the doors of opportunity closed roughly in his face (DuBois, 1903).

Although I knew that you would both experience it, I wanted to expose you to spaces where you could see yourself – I wanted you to have a mirror in this world that reflected you as well as a door to which you could open and access the tools to ensure your success.

As a child, this double consciousness caused me to code switch often. I would jokingly say that I could fit in on Wall Street and MLK Boulevard, but what this did to my psyche was problematic. For you, I hope that you will be comfortable enough in yourselves that you will not have the need to code switch, and that you will just be you – on any street – in any setting.

I have now reached the point in my life where I am not code switching for anyone. I am unapologetically me in all my imperfections and all my glory – no matter what. I want you to reach that point to as you navigate through this world realizing that you may as well be you and not aspire to change who you are to fit into someone you are not to make the dominant culture feel comfortable.

Unfortunately, the double consciousness does not dissipate as you get older, but the way you learn to navigate it does.

First, be comfortable with your greatness no matter who you are around knowing that although society is uncomfortable with your prominence, you have to remain true to who you are.

We chose to put you in a more diverse district, so you could see yourself and be seen. There were challenges there are well.

Like the time you came home saying,

"Mom, the kids at school said I act white because I do my work, the way I talk, and because of how I dress."

It saddened me as I thought back to my own experience of attending school in the inner city and being told that I "act white" or being made to feel somehow that I did not love my Blackness because I wanted to show my excellence and strive for more.

When the kids asked you if we were still married and your response yielded a,

"Yep, you're White" reply, I knew we had to have a conversation.

We want you both to be excellent at all times, to do your best, to show others what excellency looks like—to display your Black excellency.

**

Lesson 19: Let your light shine

Matthew 5:16 *In the same way, let your light shine before others, so that they may see your good works and give glory to your Father who is in heaven.*

A few weeks ago, we went to see *Queen & Slim*. The story is a riveting picture of life for people of color in 2019. In one scene, Slim asks Queen if she is a good lawyer, and she says I am an excellent lawyer. To which he asks her, why do all Black people have to be excellent, why can't we just be?

I want to clarify something to you both, and that is we want greatness from you through your ability to serve others in this life, not because you are Black, but because our Father in heaven expects it, and as your parents we demand it. Does that place a level of expectancy on you to do your best – yes, it does, but I always want you to let your light shine. We also want you to know that what it takes for you to excel is different for others, so do not measure yourself against others – be great for you! In the same sense, I want you both to know that you are enough!

We do not aspire to greatness to prove ourselves worthy; we do it because that is how we are wired – you are not trying to outdo anyone, but yourself. You owe it to yourself to be great because if you are trying to be something for a world that at present has counted you out – you lost already.

**

We want you to be proud of who you are, where you come from, and never to dim your light for anyone.

I want you to know that for years, Black youth have been accused of "acting white." Economist Roland Fryer (who happens to be the youngest African-American professor to receive tenure at Harvard) defines this simply as any "statistically significant racial differences in relationship between popularity and grades" (Fryer, Torelli, 2005).

In our community, acting white can mean taking AP classes, speaking proper English, hanging around white people, or not dressing a certain way. When you aspire to excellence, you can be accused of thinking you're "better" than the other students of color, or acting as though you have forgotten where you came from.

**

Lesson 20: Better Off, Not Than

I do not ever want you to look down on anyone as you navigate
this world. When we were coming up, we had it rough, went to bed
hungry most nights, and had utilities cut off often. Others would
look down on our situation or make us feel like we were not good
enough, and we are not raising you in that way.

We want you to know that we have worked hard to give you more
so that you would never know the feeling of going to sleep with an
empty belly so that you would not know the feeling of needing
candlelight to see, or that you would not have to boil water on the
stove in order to take a hot bath.

We did not work hard so you could look down on those who may
have it worse than you. Life is funny in that you never know what
the cards can deal to you. Life has dealt you a hand in which you
may be better off than some people, but remember you are not
better than anyone else. There is a difference.

**

I want you both to learn about authors that reflect who you are, like
Langston Hughes, Mildred Taylor, W.E.B. Du Bois, Ralph Ellison,
Zora Neale Hurston, Ta-Nehisi Coates, Tupac Shakur and many
others. Remember that you are excellent. You are kings and
queens, and learning is not something that is reserved for those
who ae white, but it is yours for the taking!

Watching your grades decline in an effort to fit in with those kids
who told you that you were acting white for being respectful and
doing your work was a letdown for me as a parent and as an

educator. I watched you try to fit in so badly that you were willing to pretend to be less than who you are.

I tell you these things because I have watched it too many times in my classroom. And just as I refuse to sit back and allow it to happen with my students, I will not let it happen in my home.

We still fight through this today. I constantly have to stay on top of your grades and work with you to catch back up on your missing work and assignments.

I also seek to do something else with you which is to talk about why you even have the right to have the audacity to get an education.

We understand as parents that our history is what makes us who we are, and we immerse you in it whenever we can. You were so young when we went to the Lorraine Motel where we talked about the Edmund Pettus Bridge where leaders like Rep. John Lewis and Dr. Martin Luther King Jr. were nearly beaten to death so that I could become a teacher years later and teach children of all races, and eventually become the first person of color to be chosen as the Teacher of the Year for my state.

(You with Congressman John Lewis)

They marched across that bridge so that you, and all our beautiful kings and queens, can be who they want to be. They marched across that bridge so that there could be a Barack and Michelle Obama, a Jay-Z and Beyoncé, an Oprah, a you and a me, and so that you can aspire to greatness!

Not only did we take you to those museums, but you met with Congressman John Lewis. He told you, as you both looked at the picture of him, Reverend Abernathy, Coretta Scott King, Martin Luther King, Jr., and Hosea Williams marching on Washington,

"I am the last living person from this picture. They are all gone."

He spent another 30 minutes with you showing you all of his pictures and telling you that you could be anything and go anywhere. We gave you access to not only secondary but to primary sources.

We often talk with you both about Brown vs. the Board of

Education and how this case allows you to go to desegregated schools and made law the fact that "separate but equal" has no place," and that segregated schools are "inherently unequal".

Please know that we do this because we love you. We love you just the way you are. I know we are hard on you, and we make you both feel like you can't just be "normal" – but I want you to aspire to greatness because you have that right now – because, as John Lewis so eloquently reminded you, the people who have paved the way for you "they are gone", and we are in their service to do the right thing with the opportunities we have been given.

To be quite honest, I love every child, which is why I have devoted my adult life to be in the service of them. I understood that as an educator, I had to set high expectations for all students so that all children could perceive that they can and should aspire to be all that they can be.

I want you both to know that because of your skin color, you will have an insurmountable amount of pressure in life, from societal pressure, to implicit bias, to a lack of belief, to microaggressions, and finally from our own kinfolk who will sometimes perceive your desire to be excellent as a departure from Blackness. I hope we will stop inflicting pain upon our own people because the world places enough pain on us all on its own.

Early in my career, I told myself that I wanted to go where the need was the greatest, and I hope you both will aspire to do the same. We often think that we have to do something grandiose in this world, but I want you both to know that, as Martin Luther King Jr. said, you can be great through your service to others.

**

Lesson 21: Servant Leadership

Servant leadership is defined as a feeling of wanting to serve and that feeling of wanting to serve leading to an urge to lead (Greenleaf, 1977). In this definition, the desire to serve is above the desire to lead.

My first official experience as a leader was when I was 23 years old as a platoon sergeant in the military. Being so young and having 30 soldiers under my charge, I always felt as if I had to prove myself. My soldiers ranged in age from 18 to 45 years old. Not only did I have to deal with being a female in charge, but I was Black, and I was young.

In that role, what propelled me towards success was that I embraced servant leadership, and committed to the tenets of Loyalty, Duty, Respect, Selfless Service, Honor, Integrity, and Personal Courage (LDRSHIP) that I learned in the military. I pass them to you:

1. Loyalty: Always be loyal to the mission, the people, and the organization you are serving. As you get older never forget who you are and remain loyal to your core beliefs. Loyalty can manifest as staying later, arriving earlier, and seeing projects to completion no matter how difficult they may be. Loyalty also means that you are more concerned with the needs of others above your own.

2. Duty: Duty refers to service as well and a leader's duty to others and to serve others. In relation to servant leadership, duty is an obligation and responsibility of the leader. As our children, it is your duty to listen and be respectful to us. Obedience is vital.

3. Respect: A servant leader is respectful of themselves and

97

others. This respect impacts those who follow in that the leader honors the expertise of others and recognizes that everyone has something to contribute.

4. Selfless Service: A servant leader understands that service is all about others. I often share with the people that I lead that being a servant leader is like dying daily to yourself. Being a mother is like a daily death as well. I know that sounds very dramatic, but I am not speaking of a literal death, but a figurative death. I die to my desires, and seek to meet yours. With selfless service, it is not about your wants or your needs, but what is the best outcome for the vision, mission, and goal you are trying to achieve.

5. Honor: In everything we do, we should do it in a way that brings honor and prestige to what we stand for. Having honor also means adhering to what is right. I recently was faced with a situation where I needed to make a formal report about a situation I was made aware of. I thought about the potential fall out and the repercussions that would ensue because someone had been derelict in their duties. I understood that there could be a negative impact on a number of people, but because I strive to be honorable in my service, I knew that I must always toe the line of righteousness and truth. As you grow up and have opportunities to lead, you will be faced with these situations on a day to day basis, but you must always aspire to remain on the right side of truth. The Bible also speaks about honoring us as your parents (Exodus 20:12 - *Honor your father and your mother, that your days may be long upon the land which the LORD your God is giving you*). I want you to understand that the Lord does not tell you to love us or to respect us because to honor someone is to

Kelisa Wing   If I Could

esteem them, which embodies respect, reverence, and love all in one.

6. Integrity: This has been one of the most important of the leadership attributes for me, and I hope you take heed to it as you continue to grow. Many people understand integrity to mean that a person is honest and has impenetrable moral principles; however, I believe that being an integritous person also speaks to a state of being whole. No matter who it separates you from or brings you to, you have to always stand on truth. A servant leader, at the very core of who they are, must espouse values of integrity and honesty. People need to know that you are morally principled. Your word is your bond, pledge, and your vow.

7. Personal Courage: Personal Courage not only speaks for physical courage, but it also pertains to moral courage. It takes courage to not be fearful in uncomfortable situations.

**

This school year, you both got the opportunity to have a teacher of color, and it has made all the difference this year with the amount of belief that your 2nd grade teacher has placed in you. While some teachers would have viewed your busyness as a problem, your teacher requested for you to be in Student Council, as she saw leadership skills in you that needed to be honed through a positive experience.

She told me that she would do everything to ensure your success. According to a UConn study, "Having just one Black teacher in elementary school not only makes children more likely to graduate high school – it also makes them significantly more likely to enroll in college" (Enright & Rosen, 2018).

I look around your classroom, and I see you sitting at a table with children wearing yamakas and hijabs. When you come home and talk to me about Ramadan and Diwali, I know that we made the best decision to place you in the school with more diversity as opposed to higher test scores.

At your parent teacher conference, tears welled in my eyes as your teacher talked about the challenges of raising Black boys. I know that she is uniquely experienced to know what you need and to be culturally relevant to your learning style. She reinforces the idea that you can be great.

You both can be great by being good people, and by serving others you become infinitely great!

Part VI: Your Gift will Make Room for You

Part VI: Your Gift Will Make Room for You

It is almost 2020, and we are only almost 55 years beyond the Civil Rights Act being enacted. 55 years ago – a few years after your grandparents were born, and only 15 years before I was born.

I get so angry when people want to know why we cannot "move on". It has not been that long ago that we were not legally afforded the same rights as everyone else.

My parents did not talk with us about finances. Our conversations centered around doing well in school so that we could do well in life, but as far as how to manage funds, I had to learn about financial literacy on my own. For their generation, and the generations that came before them, they were just trying to make it.

My parents were just young children when the Civil Rights Act was passed into law. You have to understand that the ability to produce and generate wealth up until that point for people of color was difficult. Lyndon Johnson, the 36th President said,

You do not take a person who, for years, has been hobbled by chains and liberate him, bring him up to the starting line of a race and then say, 'You are free to compete with all the others,' and still justly believe that you have been completely fair. Thus it is not

103

enough just to open the gates of opportunity. All our citizens must have the ability to walk through those gates (1965).

What President Johnson was underscoring was that in 1965, we had not been given the same opportunities as others had. What other people had acquired up until that point and had been able to pass on to the next generation in their lineage, we had not had that luxury to do. When I was growing up in the 80s and 90s, we were trying to make it.

It did not help that the government flooded the inner city with drugs and passed laws that funneled Black people from their families into prison. These things continued to push us further back on the proverbial starting line that Lyndon Johnson spoke of at Howard.

As a kid, we struggled with money in that we seemed to never have enough. Many of the decisions that were made in our household was out of survival. My mother struggled each month with the following choices: *Do we pay this heating bill or the water bill? Should we pay the mortgage or the car note? Do we buy groceries or pay the light bill?*

Each month, I watched your Nana have to make decisions to survive from month to month. I watched her work to pay bills until eventually, she could not sustain that lifestyle, and the bank seized our house and any other assets they could take.

Watching this play out as a child has had a profound impact on my life, and I vowed to never be broke and to aspire to live a life that was not going to be pay check to pay check.

I want you both to do better than your father and I. We are doing okay, but understand that we can do better. We want you to learn about stocks, investments, and how to diversify your portfolio.

I purposely sit you both down and talk to you about the bills, how I manage the budget in the house, and the importance of saving. I want you to know how much the mortgage, car note, and utility bills are so you understand that nothing in life is free. I want you to be financially literate and to have the skills and knowledge that will allow you both to make informed and effective decisions with all of your financial resources.

I want you both to build up generational wealth that you can pass along to your children and your children's children. I want you both to understand the value of a dollar. Things depreciate, so don't waste your money on things – invest in possessions that can appreciate with time.

Never forget our lessons on the couch when we are paying bills. I showed you those things so that you could be wiser than I ever was, so that you could build a legacy for our next generation through financial literacy and fiscal responsibility.

I work hard for our family to show you how to survive within a system that was not set up for us to be successful. I show you how to put yourself out there, take risks, grow through failure, and be vulnerable in an effort to show you how to hustle and grind through this thing we call life.

While you both will need a career in order to make money and be successful, I want you to understand that if you discover your passion and use the skills that are already embedded on the inside of you, you will never feel like you are working a day in your life.

People often ask me how I can do all I do with the time constraints that life places on us, but I want you both to know that you make time for what you want. If you want to be successful and effective, you have to make the time for it. Proverbs 18:16 says *A man's gift makes room for him, And brings him before great men.* Learn to use your gifts to your advantage.

I live this out loud for you both to see, but you have to remember to use the gifts you have because they are from God and for His glory. If you exercise them, they can bring you great success.

I used to wonder why I always felt the need to write and read. I could not get enough of it in my youth; however, it was not what everyone else was doing and at times it made me seem odd. I was also drawn to increasing mine and others' awareness of the plights of those who were underrepresented.

I would write editorials in the school newspaper so that I could learn more through the process. I was often surprised and humbled (and I still am today) to learn that people actually wanted to hear what I had to say. I would study activists like Martin Luther King, Jr., Malcom X, and even Henry David Thoreau to understand the differences between civil disobedience and the "by any means necessary" approach that some of our great leaders espoused.

I never thought I had something that was worth sharing with the world, I was simply working the gifts that I was given, and He has used those gifts to bring awareness to you and others. I never imagined that my desire to consume literacy would take me to the places I have seen. I was only being obedient to my calling.

I want you both to harness your gifts and allow them to take you before great men because the more you exercise your gift, the more impact your gift makes, and the more impact that it makes, the more others will take notice of your gifts. You will be amazed at the doors that will be opened – and the people your gifts will bring in your presence.

Part VII: F.E.A.R.

(Forget Everything and Run or Face Everything and Rise)

Part VII: F.E.A.R

(Forget Everything and Run or Face Everything and Rise)

As I pen this final chapter of this book, our country is getting ready to enter a new decade. So much has happened in the last few years since you both entered the world.

To our shock, the 45th President was elected. I remember that night all too clearly. I went into my closet and sobbed in disbelief because I knew that I had to meet this man since I was my state's Teacher of the Year. It was no secret how he felt about people of color, immigrants, or differently abled people – anyone who was not white was not welcome in 45's America.

Even his "Make America Great *Again*" campaign denoted that somehow, America had lost her greatness, but we all knew what this meant. He was peddling in the same hate that brought Hitler to prominence in the 1900s, by selling lies as truths and truths as lies, and America fell for it – hook, line, and sinker.

I remember going into my classroom the day after the election and a group of white students would not allow my Hispanic students in – they were "building a wall".

My heart broke to watch the civility that we had in our class dissipate within 24 hours because the President-elect was spreading his denigration, abhorrence, and malice.

"Ms. Wing, are you worried that the new President is going to send you back to Africa?," one of my student's asked me.

I laughed, "No, my people did not immigrate here. We were brought here and my other ancestors, the Native Americans, were already here, so I am not worried about being sent anywhere."

Although I found this exchange comical, I also found it a sad commentary on the sign of the times.

The next day, I decided to put all of my classes, all 105 of my students into a circle. We talked about why some people had darker skin and kinkier hair than others. That it was all based on how close we were to the equator and that we were created in such a way so we would be protected.

I spoke to my English class that day about Biology, melanin, and how that was the scientific reason that our skin was of a darker hue. We then began to talk about what made us similar. As I looked around that circle, I realized that it did not matter what the President-elect would do when he took office in January 2017, what mattered was that I would remember everything I had been taught over the years and face these trying times with a mind full of knowledge and a heart full of love.

I gave my students an assignment to either write the President-elect a letter giving him advice on how to bring the country together, or they could write President Obama a letter as he was preparing to leave the White House.

Overwhelmingly, my students wrote President Obama letters thanking him for all he did over the course of his time in office. I won't sit here and pretend that he always got things right, but he brought civility to the office, and he was always presidential when it mattered, which is much more than I can say for these current times.

Right before he left office, to my students' surprise, President Obama actually took the time to write my students back:

THE WHITE HOUSE
WASHINGTON

January 15, 2017

Ms. Wing's Class
Faith Middle School
Fort Mitchell, Alabama

Dear Students:

Thank you for writing. Hearing from young people like you inspires me each and every day, and I am glad you took the time to share your thoughts.

As a Nation, we have no higher priority than making sure the doors of opportunity are wide open for you and your generation. And as your President, that is a promise I will never stop working to keep.

In the years ahead, always remember that nothing is beyond your reach as long as you are willing to dream big and work hard. If you stay focused on your education, I know there are no limits to what you can achieve.

Thank you, again, for your kind note. I wish you all the best.

Sincerely,

I was just as surprised as my students. The lesson they learned was that they can make a difference and command the attention of the highest office in the land.

That December, I visited the Pentagon and got to meet the Under Secretary of the Army and the Secretary of the Army. I remember sitting in their office in the Pentagon. Secretary Fanning said,

"You're an English teacher, correct?"

"Yes I am." I humbly said.

He began to share with me that this was the day that they had to submit their resignation letters to President Obama.

"Much of what is in the beginning of this letter is very formal, but after the formality, we can write what we want to. What I want to know is how do I express in words that it was not the position, but the ability to serve this man that was the real honor, how can I adequately express that?"

I sat there with not much to say, surprised by his candor. There was a somber aura in the Pentagon that day with all of the inhabitants understanding that things were going to be drastically changing.

When I visited the Pentagon a few months later, one of the people commented that during the previous administration, it ran like a well-oiled machine; however, it now had many vacant positions.

(Eric Fanning, 22nd Secretary of the Army)

That April, I met the President. It was a somber day for many of us based on the exclusionary practices that he had already undertaken since taking office, but I knew that I was there representing something much bigger than myself. I was there on behalf of all of the other teachers across the nation who have dedicated themselves to be in the service of children just as I had.

I walked into the Oval Office that day with you both on my mind. The entire bus ride there, I listened to "Redbone" by Childish Gambino. The melodic beat eerily playing through my headphones with the verse on repeat,

> *But stay woke*
> *They be creepin'*
> *They gon' find you*
> *Gon' catch you sleepin' (oh)*

loudly reverberating through my eardrums as we pulled closer and closer to 1600 Pennsylvania Avenue.

After we disembarked from the bus, so many things happened. Certain family members of the teachers of the year were mistreated because of their immigrant status as well as teachers of the year. It felt like we were watching it on a television as opposed to seeing it in living color.

When I walked into the Oval Office, I looked up at the ceiling and took note of the rug that lie on the floor in front of the desk. I wondered how the previous occupants must have paced around that carpet as they were faced with difficult decisions.

I let my fingers glide over the desk and paused at the sharp corner. My emotions were all over the place in the room. There were bright lights with all of the cameras flashing and the noise of those around me.

When my friend Abdul asked if we could sing "Lift Every Voice and Sing", I was snapped back into the moment (McLaughlin, 2018) . I clearly remember looking back and forth at the President then Abdul and back at the President.

My mouth hung open waiting for his answer,

"Sure," I thought, *he has absolutely no idea what this song is.*

It was as though I blacked out. I thought about all those we lost to senseless violence. I thought about not feeling like we belonged. I thought about raising you both and keeping you safe.

Lift every voice and sing
Till earth and heaven ring
Ring with the harmonies of Liberty
Let our rejoicing rise
High as the list'ning skies, let it resound loud as the rolling sea
Sing a song full of faith that the dark past has taught us
Sing a song full of the hope that the present has brought us
Facing the rising sun of our new day begun

Let us march on till victory is won (Johnson, 1917)

When I opened my eyes, the President said,

"Oh my God, her voice! Did you hear her voice!!! Wow, what a voice!!!," He said as he clapped slowly and loudly.

(April 2017)

I still do not believe that he knows what happened in that room that day, but I will never forget it. To sing "Lift Every Voice and Sing" in the Oval Office, to that President, under those circumstances was a memory that I will cherish forever.

This song marked the liberation and freedom of Black people – that later became known as the Black National Anthem. It truly was a proud moment for those who truly comprehended the magnitude and significance of the moment.

Since that time, we have watched the administration ban Muslims from the country. We have witnessed the President refer to countries with people who look like us in dehumanizing, denigrating, and derogatory terms. We have seen children locked in cages and separated from their parents at the borders.

My heart broke the day I saw a father drown trying to save his daughter as they attempted to come into this country. Him and his beautiful daughter laid lifeless in the water just trying to obtain the "American dream". Unlike we were told by the President, he was not "bringing drugs", guns, or anything else. He was bringing his hopes, dreams, and desire for a better life.

We have had countless mass shootings with no resolution from the administration on gun violence. We have witnessed this administration try to destroy all the policies of the previous one at the expense of others. We have sat back in awe watching relationships that we built over decades with other world leaders being torn down in a matter of two years.

When Stephon Clark was shot seven times after having 20 rounds fired at him with his hands up, the President refused to take action, saying that it was a "local issue" (Reilly, 2018) even though it continues to happen nationally.

We have listened with disdain while the President defends racists and vilifies people of color, even saying, "You also had very fine people on both sides" (Shafer, 2019), while describing neo-Nazis and white nationalists.

We have watched his insidious hate-fueled rhetoric bring out the worst in this society, and even read a Manifesto from a murderer in El Paso, TX quote the President as a motivating factor for killing our Hispanic brothers and sisters.

And through it all, I ask for you both to continue to love people, to continue to see the good around you, to live a life where you model the world you want to see reflected back at you. I know that I am asking a lot.

The Bible reminds us in Matthew 5: 43-48

[43] You have heard that it was said, 'You shall love your neighbor and hate your enemy.' [44] But I say to you, Love your enemies and pray for those who persecute you, [45] so that you may be sons of your Father who is in heaven. For He makes His sun rise on the evil and on the good, and sends rain on the just and on the unjust. [46] For if you love those who love you, what reward do you have? Do not even the tax collectors do the same? [47] And if you greet only your brothers, what more are you doing than others? Do not even the Gentiles do the same? [48] You therefore must be perfect, as your heavenly Father is perfect.

As you go out into the world, you are going to be faced with people who will disagree with you for no other reason than to simply disagree. There will be people who will not like you for no other reason than the fact that they simply do not like you. Does it make it right, no, but you cannot control them. All you can do is control how you respond to them.

The truth of the matter is that although I abhor the behavior and actions the President takes, I pray for our President and anyone who is in a leadership position. I understand that in this life nothing happens by happenstance or circumstance. Everything is either ordained or allowed. So I trust God's plan – I ask you to do that as well. I have to believe that there is a lesson in all of this – just as I have taught you to learn from every good and bad experience.

The bottom line is, it really does not matter who is in charge of this nation, who is in Congress, or who is in the Senate – what matters is that you know who you are. What matters to me is that you remember everything you have learned over the years, and that you make good decisions. What matters is that you are a good person and that you are good to people. What matters is that you face everything that comes your way with boldness and confidence.

I share these lessons with you both to encourage you to do hard things and to not go through life in fear.

When I became your mother, I worried about what would happen when you are no longer under my care or when you leave our home, but I have decided to face everything and rise.

I carry inside of me the knowledge that my grandmother and my mother gave to me, and their mothers gave to them, and I pass it to you. No matter how much I worry or stress, I have to trust that everything I have placed in you – everything that I will *continue* place in you, that you will listen, adhere, and apply it.

There are so many things I cannot keep you from, but we will face everything together. I will arm you with knowledge, love, and truth because I want you to rise in life. Rise above the hate that you will encounter. Rise above the drama that will come your way. Rise above pettiness, evil, and injustice – and face it all head on.

I do not know what the future holds for you both. I pray that you will take every lesson, every conversation, every bit of advice, and use it to your advantage.

I will not sit here and tell you that life will be easy because it will not. You will face hurt, you will be hurt, and you will cause hurt. You will have your heart broken and you will break hearts.

My hope for you is that you remember who you are – that you will rise above what society says about you – and that your greatness and your excellency will shine through.

As you continue to engage in this world, it is easy to let it overwhelm you and to cause you to be fearful, which is why personal courage is so important.

I cannot begin to describe my love for you – I want so much more for you than you could ever want for yourself, and, should you become parents, you will never understand the depths of my love for you. You often ask me what can you give to me, and the best thing you could give to me is your effort. I want to see you win!

Be safe, bold, encouraged, and be you as you continue to grow in this world. As careful as you may be, I know that I cannot stop the world from being what it is, but at the same time, I need you to stop to see the beauty. Pause and know that this world is nuanced, complex, unpredictable, and at the same time it is beautiful, astonishing, and wondrous.

If I knew
I'd try to change the world
I brought you to
Now there Isn't much more
That I can do
But I would If I could (Belle, 1992)

Always know, no matter if I am here or not, my lessons will live on through you – and you will pass them on to those who come after you. In that way, we never really leave – we plant seeds in others through our service, through our words, through our actions, and through our legacy -

We live on....

Love,

Mom

119

Epilogue

1. De'von Bailey

2. Christopher Whitfield

3. Eric Logan

4. Jamarion Robinson

5. JaQuavion Slaton

6. Ryan Twyman

7. Brandon Webber

8. Jimmy Atchison

9. Willie McCoy

10. Emantic Fitzgerald Bradford Jr.

11. D'Ettrick Griffin

12. Jemel Roberson

13. DeAndre Ballard

14. Botham Jean

15. Robert Lawrence White

16. Romarley Graham

17. Manual Loggins Jr.

18. Wendall Allen

19. Kendrec McDade

20. Larry Jackson, Jr.

21. Jonathan Ferrell

22. Jordan Baker

23. Victor White III

24. Dontre Hamilton

25. Kajime Powell

26. Rumain Brisbon

27. Charly Keunang

28. Tony Robinson

29. Brendon Glenn

30. Samuel DuBose

31. Christian Taylor

32. Jamar Clark

33. Mario Woods

34. Quintonio LeGrier

35. Gregory Gunn

36. Akiel Denkins

37. Terrance Sterling

38. Terence Crutcher

39. Keith Lamont Scott

40. Alfred Olango

41. Jordan Edwards

42. Danny Ray Thomas

43. DeJuan Guillory

44. Patrick Harmon

45. Jonathan Hart

46. Maurice Granton

47. Julius Johnson

Thank you for taking this journey with me through this book. These are just some of the names of the people who have been killed by police officers since my children were born. If I added all the names, I could have filled the pages of this book. I want you to know that there are thousands more. Some of them were the same age as my children, and some of them younger than they are. I hope you will go back and read their names aloud. I do not share their names with you to shock you, but to ensure that you learn about them; they are a part of our history too.

With social media, many of their names were turned into a trending hashtag, but they were so much more than that. Some of them were killed trying to protect others and mistook as the perpetrators. Some of them were killed seeking the help of the officers. Most of them were unarmed, and many of their killers were found not guilty or not even charged in the first place. There are many families still seeking justice for their senseless murders.

Why is it that white mass murderers are typically arrested without incident, yet people of color, unarmed, are not? Why is it that 1 in 1,000 Black people are likely to be killed by police officers as opposed to 1 in 100,000 for white people (Mock, 2019)? These are all the questions I hope you will ask and seek to find answers and solutions for.

Stop being distracted by things that are not important to the larger issues that besiege this country. Stop buying into the lies and the distractions. Understand that when John Carlos and Tommie Smith raised their fists in the 1968 Summer Olympics it was about social justice just as it is when an NFL player kneels. When Colin started kneeling, it was never about "disrespecting" a flag or a lack of love for this country, but it was always about the people you have read about in this book - the people we lost throughout history due to injustices, and the lives that never really mattered in this country. It is about feeling systemized, marginalized, and victimized for the color of your skin.

It is about not being allowed to live a life without judgement. It is about my son, who at six years old was criminalized at school and questioned with no due process, no notification, and no assumption of innocence – introduced to the injustice system way too soon. It is about white women calling the police on Black children at the neighborhood pool. It is about a white woman in Brooklyn who called the police on a 7 year old Black boy who she falsely accused of "touching her butt" – only to later find out it was his book bag that bumped into her. It is about a Black Grad student at Yale who dozed off in a dorm after working diligently to complete her work who had the police called on her; it is about the two Black men who were arrested for sitting in Starbucks in Philly; it is about a Black man who had the police called on him in Ohio for cashing a check at a bank. It is about a white woman who called the police on Black people for having a barbeque in the park. Finally, it is about a soldier in the US Army who had a gun pulled out on her and her friends at a convenience store in Kentucky and told "we don't serve your kind here" the day after 9/11/2001 – my heart sank to the pit of my stomach knowing, in that moment as I stared down the barrel of his gun, that I was serving a country that would not serve or accept me all because of what I looked like.

125

All these things happen on a daily basis to people of color – living while Black. We cannot pretend it does not happen nor can we sit idly by anymore and choose to not talk about it to shield fragile feelings.

"Not everything that is faced can be changed, but nothing can be changed until it is faced" – James Baldwin

Will you face it with me? In addition to your thoughts and your prayers, will you act? Will you raise awareness? Will you read and educate yourselves? Will you allow yourselves to settle into a state of discomfort? Will you challenge others to face biases – both implicit and explicit? Will you unpack words and dig deep into definitions? Will you speak up, speak out, and speak against all forms of injustice no matter who it divides you from or connects you to?

If I could, I would change the world that we all have inherited. I would stop all forms of violence, and I would shield hearts. But I cannot. All I can do is to continue to share knowledge with the world through my voice, written and spoken, and continue to love others.

Tupac Shakur said,

I'm not saying I'm going to rule the world or I'm going to change the world. But I guarantee I will spark the brain that will change the world. That's our job – to spark somebody else watching us.

I want you to know that you can do anything as long as you stay humble, stay hopeful, and stay you in this thing we call life – WE can change this world.

Bibliography

Belle, R. (1992). "If I Could".

CNN Library. (2019). "Hurricane Katrina Statistics Fast Facts". https://www.cnn.com/2013/08/23/us/hurricane-katrina-statistics-fast-facts/index.html

Du Bois, W. E. B. (1903). *The Souls of Black Folk*. New York: Dover Publications.

"Emmett Till is Murdered". (2010). This Day in History. https://www.history.com/this-day-in-history.com/the-death-of-emmett-till

Enright, M. & Rosen, J. (2018). "Black Students Who Have One Black Teacher Are More Likely To Go To College". UConn Today. https://today.uconn.edu/2018/11/black-students-one-black-teacher-likely-go-college/#

Fryer, R. & Torelli, P. (2005). *An Empirical Analysis of 'Acting White'*. National Bureau of Economic Research. http://www.nber.org/papers/w11334

Greenleaf, R. K. (1977). *Servant Leadership: A Journey into the Nature of Legitimate Power and Greatness*. New York: Paulist Press.

Johnson, J. W. (1917). *Lift Every Voice and Sing*.

Johnson, L. (1965). "To Fulfill These Rights". Howard University Speech.

King, Martin Luther, Jr. (1968). "The Drum Major Instinct". https://kinginstitute.stanford.edu/king-papers/documents/drum-

McLaughlin, S. (2018). "MN teacher leads 'Lift Every Voice and Sing' in the Oval Office". https://bringmethenews.com/news/mn-teacher-leads-lift-every-voice-sing-oval-office

Mock, B. (2019). "What New Research Says About Race and Police Shootings". CityLab. www.citylab.com

NCES. (2018). Characteristics of Public School Teachers. https://nces.ed.gov/programs/coe/indicator_clr.asp

Oleszczuk, L. (2012). "Divorce Rate Among Afghanistan, Iraq War Vets Increases by 42 Percent". Christian Post. https://www.christianpost.com/news/divorce-rate-among-afghanistan-iraq-war-vets-hits-42-percent.html

Reilly, K. (2018). "Trump White House Calls Fatal Police Shooting of Stephon Clark a 'Local Matter'".

Riotta, C. (2016) "Alton Sterling is the 114th Known Black Man Killed by Police in the US in 2016". Mic.

Shafer, J. (2019). "How Trump Changed After Charlottesville". Politico Magazine. https://www.politico.com/magazine/story/2019/07/18/donald-trump-racist-rally-227408

Terry, J. (2015). "10 Years Ago Today, Kanye West said, 'George Bush Doesn't Care About Black People'". Chicago Tribune. https://www.chicagotribune.com/redeye/redeye-kanye-west-katrina-telethon-george-bush-black-people-20150902-htmlstory.html

The Holy Bible, King James Version. (1999). New York:

American Bible Society.

Washington, J. (2019). "Aiyana Stanley-Jones' Family Settles with the City of Detroit for $8 Million". *Ebony*.

THANK YOU

I started to skip a "Thank You" page in this book because I wanted it to be completely dedicated to my children; however, as this book evolved, I realized I would be remiss not to stop, pause, and say thank you to those who made this book a reality. 2019 was a struggle both personally and professionally. I faced some of the most difficult situations head on, and somehow, in spite of the plots, ploys, and plans of the enemy, I came out of it all stronger, wiser, and better.

First, I have to thank God. When I first started writing this book, I had the life knocked out of me due to unforeseen circumstances. I thought my life was over, and I could not go on. I had no motivation some days to get out of the bed, let alone to write a book. However, I learned through the pain that God's love is unchanging, and He gives you beauty for ashes. The energy to push forward and complete this necessary work for not only my children, but for others, came from God alone. I thank Him for finding favor in me to allow me to become a mother and for placing words inside of me that I am able to share with others.

To my husband, thank you for being my partner and supporting my aspirations. You unselfishly stand by my side while I am out front without a mumbling word. It takes a special kind of humility to allow me to share myself with others – for that I say thank you; I love you. You see me for who I am and you still love me. Love is the quiet understanding and acceptance of imperfection – thank you for always loving me and thank you for being the father of our children.

To my children – this entire book is my love in prose to you. I hope you appreciate it and know that you are loved.

To my mom, many of the lessons I am able to give to my children, I got them from you. You are the best mother a daughter could ask for. My love for you knows no depths nor heights – there is no ceiling or floor – no beginning and no end.

To my other parents, Dad, Wanda, and Chuck – I love you. To my mother and father in law – we love you very much. We will forever miss you JW.

Shenee you have held me up in this difficult year. I am so blessed that God not only gave me a sister, but he gave me a best friend in you. Stevie I love you big brother. To my brothers and sisters in law – I love you.

To my spiritual leaders: Apostle Townsend and Pastor Debbie Townsend – we appreciate you and still live by your Godly teaching day in and day out. We are also grateful for Bishop Grier who has preached us through some trying times over the past year.

To Sharif El-Mekki words seem to not be enough to thank you for your contribution to this body of work. I am grateful for what you do for the culture, people, and cause. I am honored to share space with you in this important fight for social justice.

To my friends and other family members – thank you for your role in my life – I am because you are!

ABOUT THE AUTHOR

Kelisa Wing has been in education for 14 years. Her journey into the teaching profession began after she was honorably discharged from the United States Army. She served as a Youth Consultant for the Self-Expression Teen Theater (SETT) under United Way. After moving to Germany with her family, she began substitute teaching, then transitioned to a Special Education paraprofessional, was a school secretary, and eventually, an Administrative Officer. She then taught 8th-grade Language Arts and Reading to military-connected children at Faith Middle School in Fort Benning, Georgia, has been an Elementary School Assistant Principal in New York, and is now a Professional Development Specialist in Virginia.

Kelisa honorably served in the U.S. Army for six years and attained the rank of Staff Sergeant. She is the author of *Conversations* (2006), *Weeds & Seeds: How To Stay Positive in the Midst of Life's Storms* (2017), *Promises and Possibilities: Dismantling the School to Prison Pipeline* (2018), and a contributing author of *Becoming a Globally Competent Teacher* (2019).

She is a 2017 State Teacher of the Year, a 2016 Association of Supervision, Curriculum, and Development (ASCD) Emerging Leader, and the 2017 University of Maryland University College (UMUC) Edward Parnell Outstanding Alumnus of the Year. She is the only educator on the Education Civil Rights Alliance (ECRA) Steering Committee, and a member of the Leading Educator Ambassadors for Equity (LEAE) with ECRA. As a member of the National Network of State Teachers of the Year (NNSTOY), she has led efforts for mentoring teacher leaders through a partnership with 100Kin10, and she is also a member of ASCD. She is also on the Advisory Board for the Learner Variability Project & Digital

Promise, ASCD's Global Advisory Council, and the ASCD College Football Playoff Foundation (CFP) Diversifying the Teacher Pipeline Working Group. She speaks both nationally and internationally about discipline reform, equity, student engagement, and many other topics

Kelisa holds a bachelor's degree in English from UMUC, a Master of Arts in Secondary Education, and an Educational Specialist degree with a concentration in Curriculum, Instruction, and Educational Leadership from the University of Phoenix.

Kelisa credits her faith in God, and His grace, favor, and mercy as the key to her success.

Kelisa lives in Northern Virginia with her husband and children.

Made in the USA
Middletown, DE
27 December 2019